Knowledge Retention
Strategies and Solutions

The Business Value of IT: Managing Risks, Optimizing Performance and Measuring Results
Michael D. S. Harris, David Herron, and Stasia Iwanicki
ISBN: 1-4200-6474-6

CISO Leadership: Essential Principles for Success
Todd Fitzgerald and Micki Krause
ISBN: 0-8493-7943-1

The Debugger's Handbook
J.F. DiMarzio
ISBN: 0-8493-8034-0

Effective Software Maintenance and Evolution: A Reuse-Based Approach
Stanislaw Jarzabek
ISBN: 0-8493-3592-2

The Ethical Hack: A Framework for Business Value Penetration Testing
James S. Tiller
ISBN: 084931609X

Implementing Electronic Document and Record Management Systems
Azad Adam
ISBN: 0-8493-8059-6

Implementing the IT Balanced Scorecard: Aligning IT with Corporate Strategy
Jessica Keyes
ISBN: 0-8493-2621-4

Information Security Cost Management
Ioana V. Bazavan and Ian Lim
ISBN: 0-8493-9275-6

The Insider's Guide to Outsourcing Risks and Rewards
Johann Rost
ISBN: 0-8493-7017-5

Interpreting the CMMI®: A Process Improvement Approach, Second Edition
Margaret K. Kulpa and Kent A. Johnson
ISBN: 1-4200-6052-X

Knowledge Management, Business Intelligence, and Content Management: The IT Practitioner's Guide
Jessica Keyes
ISBN: 0-8493-9385-X

Manage Software Testing
Peter Farrell-Vinay
ISBN: 0-8493-9383-3

Managing Global Development Risk
James M. Hussey and Steven E. Hall
ISBN: 1-4200-5520-8

Patterns for Performance and Operability: Building and Testing Enterprise Software
Chris Ford, Ido Gileadi, Sanjiv Purba, and Mike Moerman
ISBN: 1-4200-5334-5

A Practical Guide to Information Systems Strategic Planning, Second Edition
Anita Cassidy
ISBN: 0-8493-5073-5

Service-Oriented Architecture: SOA Strategy, Methodology, and Technology
James P. Lawler and H. Howell-Barber
ISBN: 1-4200-4500-8

Six Sigma Software Development, Second Edition
Christine B. Tayntor
ISBN: 1-4200-4426-5

Successful Packaged Software Implementation
Christine B. Tayntor
ISBN: 0-8493-3410-1

Knowledge Retention
Strategies and Solutions

Jay Liebowitz

CRC Press
Taylor & Francis Group
Boca Raton London New York

CRC Press is an imprint of the
Taylor & Francis Group, an **informa** business

AN AUERBACH BOOK

Auerbach Publications
Taylor & Francis Group
6000 Broken Sound Parkway NW, Suite 300
Boca Raton, FL 33487-2742

International Standard Book Number-13: 978-1-4200-6465-0 (Hardcover)

Library of Congress Cataloging-in-Publication Data

Liebowitz, Jay, 1957-
   Knowledge retention : strategies and solutions / Jay Liebowitz.
      p. cm.
   Includes bibliographical references and index.
   ISBN 978-1-4200-6465-0 (hbk. : alk. paper)
   1. Knowledge management. 2. Human capital--Management. I. Title.

HD30.2.L526 2008
658.4'038--dc22
                                                         2008014240

Visit the Taylor & Francis Web site at
http://www.taylorandfrancis.com

and the Auerbach Web site at
http://www.auerbach-publications.com

Dedication

To my Janet, Jason, Kenny, and Mom.

To the wonderful case study contributors of leading
organizations involved in knowledge retention.

To all my students and colleagues over the years.

To the Auerbach Publishing family.

And to those generations preceding us and those succeeding us.

Contents

Preface xi

Acknowledgments xiii

Author xv

Chapter 1

Setting the Stage 1
1.1   Possible Barriers to Knowledge Retention 4
1.2   Building the Corporate Memory of the Firm 6
1.3   Summary 6

Chapter 2

Determining Critical "At-Risk" Knowledge 7

Chapter 3

Easy-to-Accomplish Knowledge Retention Techniques 15
3.1   Interviews 15
3.2   Mentoring 17
      3.2.1   The Mentoring Program at Johns Hopkins
              University (JHU) 19
3.3   Oral Histories, Storytelling 19
3.4   Cheat Sheets 21
3.5   Exit Interviews 21
3.6   The Bible 22
3.7   After-Action Reviews 23
3.8   Online Communities, Wikis, Blogs, Social Networking Sites 24
Reference 24

Chapter 4

Developing a Knowledge Retention Framework 25
4.1   The Pillars of Knowledge Retention 26

4.1.1   Recognition and Reward Structure 26
4.1.2   Bidirectional Knowledge Flow 27
4.1.3   Personalization and Codification.............................28
4.1.4   The Golden Gem..28
4.2   Examples: Getting Started in Knowledge Retention.........................29
References...40

Chapter 5

Knowledge Retention: Learning from Others 41
5.1   A Short Case Study: The Knowledge Retention Program for the
Office of the Deputy Inspector General for Auditing (ODIG-AUD) 41
5.1.1   People...41
5.1.2   Process 42
5.1.3   Technology...43
5.1.4   Summary 43
5.2   Best Practices of the Private Sector and Universities for Using
Retirees as a Form of Knowledge Retention and Transfer............... 44
5.3   Other Lessons Learned in Knowledge Retention 46
5.4   Learning from Others about Lessons Learned Systems and
Processes...48
5.4.1   What Works and What Does Not................................48
5.4.2   Possible Lessons Learned: Proof of Concept Criteria 52
References...53

Chapter 6

Calculating the Loss of Knowledge 55
6.1   The "Grayout" Factor...55
6.2   Turning Knowledge Loss into a Positive Gain 58
6.3   Knowledge Retention at Tennessee Valley Authority (TVA):
Assessing Knowledge Loss 59
6.4   Summary...60
References...61

Chapter 7

Using Organizational Network Analysis to Inform
Knowledge Retention Efforts...63
7.1   Case Example: The Department Organizational Network
Analysis 64
7.1.1   Respondent Demographics...................................... 64
7.1.2   Insights Gained from the Department Organizational
Network Analysis (ONA).. 64

7.1.3 Knowledge Retention Recommendations Based on the
Department ONA.. 66
7.2 An Example of an ONA Survey Instrument 67
7.3 Knowledge Retention through the ONA Lens...............................72
References..72

Chapter 8

Case Study: Knowledge Harvesting during the Big Crew Change 73

Jeffrey E. Stemke, Knowledge Strategist, Chevron Corporation and
Larry Todd Wilson, Founder and President, Knowledge Harvesting Inc.

8.1 Business Case..74
8.2 The Learning Life Cycle 75
8.3 Knowledge Retention and Transfer Processes 75
8.4 The Role of Knowledge Harvesting 76
8.5 Case Study: Capturing and Transferring a Complex Technical
Process 78
8.5.1 Focus...79
8.5.2 Find... 80
8.5.3 Elicit...81
8.5.4 Organize, Package..82
8.5.5 Expert's Review and Comments.......................................83
8.5.6 Peers' and Stakeholders' Evaluation and Comments.............83
8.6 Chevron's Experience with Knowledge Harvesting......................... 84
8.6.1 Lessons Learned 84
8.6.2 Knowledge Harvesting—A Useful Addition to
Chevron's Knowledge Retention Toolkit 84

Chapter 9

The Aerospace Corporation Case Study 87

Stewart Sutton, Joseph Betser, Mary Hornickel, Michelle Gregorio,
Jeffery Kern, Christine Lincoln, and Jovel Crisostomo, The Aerospace
Corporation Knowledge Management Office

9.1 Introduction 87
9.2 Company Background..87
9.2.1 A History of Knowledge Retention (1960 to Present)...........88
9.2.2 The Knowledge Management Role of the Aerospace
Library and Information Resources Center 89
9.2.3 Knowledge Management within Aerospace-at-Large........... 90
9.2.3.1 1960s and 1970s... 90
9.2.3.2 1980s.. 90
9.2.3.3 1990s to 2007 91

9.3 Knowledge Management Initiatives at Aerospace 93
    9.3.1 Communities for Stewardship 94
    9.3.2 Knowledge Search 98
    9.3.3 Expertise Location 98
    9.3.4 Mission Assurance Tools and Frameworks 99
9.4 A Closer Look at Knowledge Retention Efforts 100
    9.4.1 Knowledge Retention in Communities 100
    9.4.2 Knowledge Retention in CoPs 101
    9.4.3 Community Wisdom Process (Communities of Practice [CoPs]) 101
    9.4.4 Knowledge Retention in Communities of Interest 102
    9.4.5 Community Metrics 103
    9.4.6 Technologies for Efficient Knowledge Collaboration, Capture, and Sharing 103
        9.4.6.1 Institutional Repository (Document Management) 104
        9.4.6.2 Wikis 104
        9.4.6.3 Weblogs 108
        9.4.6.4 Podcasting 108
    9.4.7 Knowledge Retention via Storytelling 109
9.5 Lessons Learned in Knowledge Retention 111
    9.5.1 A Company Library Is a Necessity for a Modern Knowledge Organization 111
    9.5.2 Knowledge Is Fragile and Needs Constant Tuning 111
    9.5.3 The Soft Stuff is the Hard Stuff 112
9.6 Summary 113
References 113

Chapter 10

Knowledge Retention: The Future 115

10.1 Cross-Generational Knowledge Flows in Edge Organizations 117
10.2 Knowledge Retention: Future Challenges 118
References 119

Index 121

Preface

With the graying workforce and the baby boomers nearing retirement, some severe human capital challenges are already facing various industry sectors, government agencies, and not-for-profits. Many organizations are looking toward knowledge management to help with their workforce development and succession planning. However, very few organizations have put knowledge retention strategies into effect in order to capture, share, and leverage this possible "lost knowledge."

This book is written to address this vacuum. It is an easy-to-read, concise guide to help organizations adopt knowledge retention strategies, techniques, and processes. The book is geared for chief human capital officers, chief learning officers, senior executives, general managers, knowledge managers, knowledge management practitioners and educators, workforce development managers, succession planning advocates, and others who play a role in the knowledge retention strategy formulation for their organizations.

The book discusses various knowledge retention issues, concepts, methods, techniques, and strategies. The book also has some selected case studies from two of the leading organizations in knowledge retention—The Aerospace Corporation and Chevron, along with Knowledge Harvesting Inc. I am indebted to these contributors who are playing influential roles in the knowledge retention area.

Jay Liebowitz, D.Sc.
Washington, D.C.

Acknowledgments

There are many people whom I would like to thank for helping me shape my ideas in this book. With the fear of leaving someone out, I will give a global round of appreciation to my students and colleagues at Johns Hopkins University, the wonderful staff at Taylor & Francis, the organizations and professionals that I have worked with over the many years in the knowledge management and knowledge retention area, and my collaborators from universities and companies here and abroad.

Of course, I owe special thanks to Janet, Jason, Kenny, and my parents, who always put a smile on my face! Enjoy!

Author

Jay Liebowitz, D.Sc., is full professor in the Carey Business School at Johns Hopkins University. He was recently ranked one of the top 10 knowledge management/ intellectual capital researchers worldwide. He is the program director of the Graduate Certificate in Competitive Intelligence at Johns Hopkins University. He is founder and editor-in-chief of *Expert Systems with Applications: An International Journal,* published by Elsevier.

Previously, Dr. Liebowitz was the first Knowledge Management Officer at National Aeronautics and Space Administration (NASA) Goddard Space Flight Center, the Robert W. Deutsch Distinguished Professor of Information Systems at the University of Maryland–Baltimore County, Chair of Artificial Intelligence at the U.S. Army War College, and Professor of Management Science at The George Washington University.

Liebowitz has published more than 35 books and over 250 articles dealing with expert/intelligent systems, knowledge management, and information technology management. His most recent books include *Making Cents Out of Knowledge Management* (Scarecrow Press, 2008), *Social Networking: The Essence of Innovation* (Scarecrow Press/Rowman & Littlefield, 2007), *Strategic Intelligence: Business Intelligence, Competitive Intelligence, and Knowledge Management* (Auerbach Publishing/Taylor & Francis, 2006), *What They Didn't Tell You about Knowledge Management* (Scarecrow Press/Rowman & Littlefield, 2006), *Communicating as IT Professionals* (Prentice Hall, 2006), and *Addressing the Human Capital Crisis in the Federal Government: A Knowledge Management Perspective* (Butterworth-Heinemann/Elsevier, 2004).

Liebowitz is the founder and chair of The World Congress on Expert Systems. He was a Fulbright Scholar, the Institute of Electrical and Electronics Engineers (IEEE)-USA Federal Communications Commission Executive Fellow, and the Computer Educator of the Year by the International Association for Computer Information Systems. He has consulted and lectured worldwide for numerous organizations, and he can be reached at jliebow1@jhu.edu.

Author

Chapter 1

Setting the Stage

Strategic human capital management has been an important area in recent years within government, industry, and academe. Strategic human capital management can be defined as the ability to be prepared, from workforce development and succession planning perspectives, in terms of having the human talent available and educated as the future workforce to meet the organization's strategic mission and vision. Simply put, it involves having the right set of people at the right time in order to meet the organization's long-term goals and vision.

Part of the reason for this growing importance of strategic human capital management is due to the demographics of our population. In many countries throughout the world, including the United States, the graying of the workforce is occurring due to the demographics of our society. The baby boomers are nearing retirement age, and changing work patterns of our younger workers have contributed to a knowledge bleed in many organizations. Because our older workers are nearing retirement and our younger workers are less likely to stay with one employer for more than a few years, it becomes paramount to find ways to best leverage and retain their knowledge before they leave the organization. In the United States federal government, for example, the President's Management Agenda was created during President George W. Bush's first term in office to address strategic management of human capital as the number one government-wide initiative of the U.S. government. The Chief Human Capital Officer was created to develop and spearhead the human capital strategy in the largest U.S. government agencies and departments. In industry, many sectors, including manufacturing, aerospace, utilities, energy, and others, are experiencing the same concerns. Even in academe, the education field is witnessing similar pangs dealing with teacher shortages and a shortage of professors in a number of technical fields, including computer science and information technology.

Before attrition takes place, organizations are trying to develop knowledge retention strategies so that critical knowledge does not walk out the door. Some organizations are conducting interviews 3 months before the employee retires, and this approach has proved ineffective. A thoughtful approach to knowledge retention should be carried out at least 2 to 3 years before a retiree becomes eligible. Better yet, a knowledge-retention strategy should be woven within the fabric of the organization from day one, because you do not know when someone will leave, and you do not know when someone will actually retire. For example, if capturing lessons learned or best practices were part of every project team's life cycle development process, then knowledge would be captured from the initial conceptual design through implementation and maintenance—that is, from the start of the project through the end date. Or linking up a mentoring or buddy system, whereby junior and senior employees are paired, can be a very effective means for sharing and leveraging knowledge.

A key point is that organizations need to be thinking from the beginning in terms of how best to capture, share, and apply knowledge so that knowledge creation and innovation can be fostered. It is not simply losing someone's knowledge if they retire or leave the organization, it is also losing their social network, if you will, in terms of who they seek out for answers to questions in their domain. Social networking, therefore, becomes an important component of the knowledge retention process. The informal networks that people create result in the creativity and "power" in the organization. The use of social network analysis to map these informal networks and knowledge flows and gaps in organizations can be a useful method to apply toward determining "relationship knowledge" (who knows who), as well as "who knows what" types of knowledge. Looking for the shortest paths between individuals (minimum geodesic distance) in order to identify the strengths of relationships is the general approach used in social network analysis.

To get started in strategic human capital management, a framework should first be established. This framework may include four key pillars: competency management, performance management, knowledge management, and change management. Competency management refers to what competencies the organization needs in its workforce of the future. Performance management deals with how best to reward or recognize people for their performance, as well as perhaps providing disincentives for those less productive. Knowledge management involves how best to capture, share, and apply knowledge in the organization to create and leverage knowledge. Change management is how to build and nurture a knowledge sharing culture whereby "sharing knowledge is power" versus the "knowledge is power" paradigm. Liebowitz in his book, *Addressing the Human Capital Crisis in the Federal Government: A Knowledge Management Perspective* (Elsevier, 2004), provides an in-depth discussion on each of these pillars.

A knowledge retention strategy should be developed and typically would fall within the knowledge management pillar. Knowledge attrition profiles in the organization should be created whereby people will have a sense for how many years they have before official retirement. IBM uses a diagnostic in terms of their "Maturing Workforce" consulting that tries to address four questions [http://www-03.ibm.com/industries/government/doc/content/bin/Maturing_Workforce_IBM1291_07_FINAL.pdf] :

1. Who will be retiring?
2. What is their business value, and what will be the impact of losing them?
3. When is this going to happen?
4. How to respond for the greatest business benefit?

Another approach may be to ask each employee the following three questions:

1. What specific area of knowledge do you possess?
2. Is there a backup expert in this area? (if so, who is it?)
3. On a scale of 1 (low) to 10 (high), how important is this knowledge area in terms of the organization's strategic vision looking 5 to 8 years down the road?

Of course, the responses would have to be vetted, perhaps by management, in order to reduce some perceptual bias. By asking the three previous questions, the organization is not limiting itself to retiree-eligibles. In fact, there may be some critical "at-risk" knowledge areas that younger employees possess, especially in the technology field, whereby the organization may be susceptible to "knowledge loss" if these individuals were to leave. Thus, this suggests the need for a comprehensive knowledge retention strategy for all different tenures in the organization.

Let us look at a quick example of an interactive advertising agency to see how they are preparing for any possible knowledge drain. They believe strongly in a collaborative environment—in fact, by virtue of their work, they have to work in collaborative teams, as different specialties are needed in order to perform the work. For example, a visual designer, interactive design specialist, and a technologist may be a team to address Web site interactive development. To encourage collaboration and knowledge sharing, people sit in open rooms whereby they are not segmented by department or specialty area. Wikis and blogs internal to the agency are in use, as well as having many shared folders based on projects, which anyone in the company can access. In addition, a phone list with people's pictures and office map locations is available on the intranet to link up with others in the agency. Additionally, having monthly breakfasts with the president and having many internal seminars open to the full agency, along with weekly company e-newsletters, help encourage a knowledge sharing environment. If someone were to leave the agency, much of the knowledge would not be lost, due to these codification and personalization approaches to knowledge retention.

NASA uses another approach to knowledge retention. Through their APPEL (Academy for Program/Project Engineering Leadership—http://appel.nasa.gov) and their NASA Engineering Network (NEN), knowledge sharing is accomplished in a number of ways. Knowledge sharing/wisdom transfer sessions are used whereby the graybeards discuss success and bittersweet stories with up-and-coming project leaders in the project management area. The Process-Based Mission Assurance Knowledge Management System (http://pbma.nasa.gov) has video nuggets of 1- to 2-minute discussions of key learnings from NASA experts across the ten NASA Centers. These are tied to the project management framework within the PBMA system. Pause and Learn (PAL) sessions are also conducted at NASA to give some introspective insight into developing reflective practitioners. The NASA Lessons Learned Information System (http://llis.nasa.gov) is another approach to acquire lessons learned during the project development life cycle.

The key issue, no matter what strategies or approaches an organization uses, is to embed knowledge retention activities within the daily working lives of the employees from the first day the employee arrives to the organization. In this manner, the organization will not be hit by surprise when the individual decides to leave the organization. More important, the organization will be building its "knowledge base" so that people can easily share, apply, learn, and create knowledge from accessing each other's corpus of knowledge.

When thinking about embedding knowledge retention activities into the daily working life, organizations are using several techniques. For example, lessons learned are captured during the project's life cycle, or at the very least, at the end of the project. Online communities are also serving as vehicles to capture, share, and leverage knowledge in various organizational core competencies. Formal mentoring programs are being used whereby the mentors and their mentees meet regularly to have knowledge exchanges about "war stories" on organizational successes and failures. The use of content management systems for storing and exchanging files is a typical application for organizations to capture information and knowledge. Bringing back retirees through emeriti programs or as specialized project team consultants can also be an effective way to share knowledge with others.

1.1 Possible Barriers to Knowledge Retention

There are a number of obstacles that organizations might face with respect to institutionalizing knowledge retention efforts. One key barrier is that people may prefer to be knowledge hoarders rather than knowledge sharers. Why would an individual want to give up his/her "competitive edge" that he/she developed over many years of experience? The answer comes down to a trust issue. There are two main types of trust: competence-based trust and benevolence-based trust. People seek out those who are competent in an area and trust their knowledge and advice. Others may be benevolent and feel altruistic for the good of the organization in sharing their knowledge with others. People want to be recognized and/or rewarded for display-ing these knowledge sharing behaviors. Thus, the human resources department, or the office of human capital management, as it is now sometimes called, has an important role to play in developing learning and knowledge sharing proficiencies to recognize and reward people for exhibiting these behaviors. This will help in breaking down the "competitive edge" issues that sometimes plague employees. Also, people are generally willing to share their knowledge if they perceive reciproc-ity in the future from the knowledge recipient.

Another obstacle to knowledge retention efforts deals with human biases in judgment. People naturally have human biases, such as the recency bias (people are influenced by recent events), causality bias (people assign cause where none exists), imaginability (people make decisions based on the way the information is presented to them), and others. These latent biases affect an individual's deci-sion-making ability and could impact knowledge that is conveyed and captured. A related phenomenon to human biases in judgment deals with the knowledge-engi-neering paradox. This paradox means that the more expert an individual, the more compiled his/her knowledge and the harder it is to extract that knowledge. Thus, a third person typically will serve as the independent party to help elicit knowledge from the individual.

A third obstacle to knowledge retention efforts is that some people may be disgruntled for some reason and decide to either not participate or sabotage the effort by giving fictitious information. In one organization, they are being asked to relocate from a nice, wooded area to a desert-like terrain. Only about 5% to 10% of the employees are expected to move to this new location. With this possible mass exodus, a knowledge-drain effect could be quite potent. This might suggest the need to capture their critical at-risk knowledge before the employees leave the organization. However, the employees may be quite annoyed about the move and may decide not to participate in the knowledge capture exercise, especially if they are quitting the organization.

A fourth obstacle to knowledge retention may be the opinion that it is impos-sible to capture 20 or 30 years of experience in 4 or 5 hours of exit interviews. This is certainly a valid complaint. This is why the knowledge retention program must be focused on specific targeted needs. For example, the knowledge retention effort may need to focus on strategic and tactical decisions that the employee typically makes as part of his/her job or focus on the social networks that the employee has built based on certain types of knowledge-related questions. Alternatively, a taxon-omy of knowledge for the organization may need to be established in order to drill down to knowledge flows and knowledge gaps for certain types of knowledge the employee possesses. We will discuss this obstacle further in forthcoming chapters.

The last key obstacle is that the knowledge retention strategy may be mis-aligned with the strategic mission of the organization. If knowledge management efforts fail, it is typically because either the knowledge management strategy was not in alignment with the strategic mission of the organization or the knowledge management program was poorly designed. The same holds true for a knowledge retention strategy. It should not be seen as being in isolation of the overall business processes. It should be seamless to the organization and be woven into the organization's fabric. If this is something else to do on top of an already full plate, then the knowledge retention program will not be successful.

1.2   Building the Corporate Memory of the Firm

A key reason for performing knowledge retention is to grow the institutional memory of the organization. In this manner, employees can learn from past successes and failures to ensure positive results. Learning from others could help avoid going down the wrong paths or reinventing the wheel.

Learning takes place at all stages of organizational development. It is not just the "graybeards" who possess the knowledge. Expertise can be possessed by younger employees as well. And it is not only at the strategic level in the organization where expertise resides, but also at the operating or tactical levels. For example, a personal assistant may know the ins and outs of getting certain paperwork approved. This administrative knowledge can be very valuable in order to get things through the pipeline.

For all these reasons, knowledge retention really must be an ongoing effort that starts at day one when the employee arrives. There should also be a variety of knowledge retention techniques applied, as "one size probably does not fit all." Both personalization ("connection") and codification ("collection") knowledge capture approaches should be used. The chapters that follow will discuss various knowledge retention strategies and approaches.

1.3   Summary

This chapter hopefully whets your appetite for engaging in knowledge retention efforts. Even though obstacles exist, many organizations are realizing that they do not have a choice in this potential knowledge-drain battle. With the baby boomers nearing retirement age and the mobility of younger workers, an organization must find ways to build its institutional memory and social networks for leveraging knowledge toward increased innovation. The knowledge management community has been preaching this notion for the past 10 years. Now organizations are waking up to the fact that they may lose their competitive edge if they do not apply knowledge management and knowledge retention efforts to stimulate collaboration and knowledge creation. The following chapters will provide a formula for success in this area.

Chapter 2

Determining Critical "At-Risk" Knowledge

The question of the day is: "How do you know what knowledge is important to capture?" An organization has multiple types of knowledge including process knowledge, strategic knowledge, relationship knowledge, and subject matter domain knowledge. Should each of these types of knowledge be captured? Specifically, what is the critical "at-risk" knowledge that affects the longevity and strategic mission of the organization?

Perhaps a calculation for an "Attention Factor" is needed in order to answer these questions. The Attention Factor should indicate what knowledge is critical to the organization and who possesses that knowledge. It could be crudely determined as follows:

Attention Factor (AF) = Knowledge Severity (KS) × Knowledge Availability (KA)

Where:

  KS = criticality of the knowledge to the strategic mission of the organization (on a scale from 1 (low) to 10 (high)).

  KA = availability of the knowledge based upon whether an expert (E) exists in the organization (1 = yes; 0 = no) and the likelihood (LE) of the expert leaving the organization in the next 5 years (on a scale from 1 [low] to 10 [high]). The aggregate KA score would be computed as E × LE.

The Attention Factor can then be ranked according to the product values between the KS and KA. For example, if the criticality of the knowledge to the strategic mission is very high and an expert exists but is nearing retirement age, then AF could be computed as:

$$AF = 10 \times (1 \times 10) = 100$$

The maximum AF score is 100. The higher the score, the greater the need for knowledge retention. Alternatively, if KS is 10 and there is no expert, the Attention Factor for knowledge retention would be zero as there is no expert in the organization for which to capture his/her knowledge.

So how do you know what knowledge is critical to the strategic mission of the organization? A quick way to determine this is to read the strategic plan for the organization and see what types of knowledge are necessary in order to carry out the strategic goals. Another source is to look at the core competencies for the organization and correspondingly check with the Human Resources (HR) department to review the human competencies needed for the organization's workforce of the future to meet these organizational core competencies.

Let us first look at the broader picture as an example. Liebowitz was involved in developing a knowledge management (KM) strategy and performance measures for the Office of Deputy Inspector General for Auditing (ODIG-AUD). A knowledge audit was conducted using the following methodology:

1. Collected documents relating to the knowledge management work at ODIG-AUD and associated critical reports (for example, ODIG-AUD Strategic Plan, etc.).
2. Developed and refined a "Knowledge Access and Sharing Survey." The survey was put into a Web-based format via Survey Tracker, and was encouraged by the Deputy Inspector General for Auditing to be completed by all ODIG-AUD employees. The survey was completed first by a pilot test group, where after final revisions were made to the survey before being fielded to all ODIG-AUD employees. We received a 65% response rate, with 464 surveys completed out of 713. We were very pleased with this response rate and were able to receive a representative sample of respondents across ODIG-AUG, as well as those based on employee length of time.
3. Conducted selected interviews with ODIG-AUD employees and ODIG-AUD customers.
4. Analyzed the survey and interview results and developed the KM strategy based on the analysis.

Through the Knowledge Management Transfer Working Group, brown-bag "lunch and learn" sessions, the KM section of the intranet site, job rotations, and a mentoring program, ODIG-AUD has been on its formal knowledge management journey. ODIG-AUD is now (appropriately) looking inwardly to best capture, share, and apply knowledge internally among its staff. The knowledge management initiatives, to be developed, relate directly to the two strategic goals of ODIG-AUD, especially Goal 2 (provide continuous improvements to ODIG-AUD operations and resources) and Objective 2 (to promote a diverse, talented, and results-oriented organization characterized by a culture of mutual trust and respect through effective communication and leadership). The knowledge management strategy will also promote workforce development and succession planning within ODIG-AUD. As such, ODIG-AUD should consider a number of key goals and initiatives as part of its knowledge management strategy:

■ Develop the organizational infrastructure to support knowledge management in ODIG-AUD. This includes developing a new position as Chief Knowledge Officer reporting to the Deputy Inspector General for Auditing, reconstituting the Knowledge Management Transfer Working Group into a formal Knowledge Management Council, appointing full-time knowledge stewards for leading and coordinating the knowledge management activities within their directorates, creating an AUDIT Retiree and Alumni Association to share successes and failures (e.g., write case studies and share with current employees), establishing a library within ODIG-AUD with a new position as library specialist, adding "learning and knowledge sharing proficiencies" to the recognition and reward system at ODIG-AUD in order to emphasize and reward people for sharing knowledge, and embedding knowledge management activities as part of everyone's daily work activities (capturing and using lessons learned/best practices during the project life cycle, having relevant "storytelling" for the first 5 to 10 minutes of staff meetings, having after-action reviews at the end of each project, etc.). Processes should also be established for capturing knowledge, such as having knowledge elicitation sessions with a knowledge engineer, posting weekly reports on the intranet and categorizing/indexing them by subject/topic area, writing down lessons learned on a weekly/monthly basis for sharing at staff meetings and posting on the intranet, exit interviews, creating compendium CDs (for example, deskbooks, such as making the transition from a GS-13 to GS-14 Program Manager), and so forth.
■ Develop the technology infrastructure (intranet) to enable knowledge sharing to take place, as well as developing quick-win pilot projects. The intranet needs to be further developed within ODIG-AUD, and appropriate resources should be allocated to ensure its development, content organization, nurturing, and maintenance (for example, the IT staff should be actively involved in the intranet's taxonomy and development). A calendar with all ODIG-AUD and related meetings (and deadlines) should be posted on the intranet, as well as having online modules and "cheat sheets" for ODIG-AUD training and how to perform various operations within ODIG-AUD. List of internal

frequently asked questions and responses, audit and external reports, Excel/ Word forms/job-related templates developed internally, local and national newspaper Web sites, and Department of Defense (DoD)-related news clips should also be included in the intranet. The Google search engine should be included as part of the intranet for both internal and Web searches. The intranet should also have links to three *essential* projects: a "yellow pages" internal "who knows what" locator system (a version of this currently exists, and it needs to be expanded and updated), a document management system, and a lessons learned/best practices system. The yellow pages should also include organizational responsibilities and subject-matter expertise. Microsoft's Sharepoint, Open Text's LiveLink (Department of Navy uses LiveLink), Plumtree/G6, EMC Documentum, Autonomy, and other software solutions should be considered as possible document management system/portal tools. The lessons learned system should also include a "push" feature to push appropriate new lessons to ODIG-AUD staff and the external community who could benefit from these lessons. Since several staff members have experience in knowing best practices to be used in ODIG-AUD (those individuals who were cited most frequently in different knowledge areas), the best practice/lessons learned system should tap the expertise of these individuals to include their best/worst practices in the system. The yellow pages project could use software like AskMe (by AskMe Corporation) or ActiveNet (Tacit Corporation) to help create the yellow pages. A longer-term project that should be undertaken by the ODIG-AUD is a Web-based, online searchable knowledge preservation project to capture the institutional knowledge of expertise in ODIG-AUD and the rationale and decision-making process for why certain decisions were made. This could be similar to NASA's Oral History Project. Additionally, data mining should be explored to develop outcomes to inform ODIG-AUD strategies.

▪ Accentuate the "personalization" approach to knowledge sharing within the ODIG-AUD. A major part of this approach is to improve intercommunications flow between teams, divisions, and directorates. Online communities of practice should be formed, with appropriate facilitators, to encourage knowledge sharing across ODIG-AUD worldwide. Cross-teaming should also be encouraged, which will enable people-to-people networking and connections to be made outside of one's own community/department and integrated across functional silos. Posting of meeting summaries, conference/ trip reports, PowerPoint slides, and the like should be put on the intranet. Knowledge sharing forums between experienced staff and those who are newer to ODIG-AUD should be conducted, as well as continuing brown-bag "learn and lunch" get-togethers. A "Weekly Reader" could be a wonderful mechanism to share information and knowledge at ODIG-AUD. A formal mentoring program should continue within ODIG-AUD, and this will also help in improving communications flow within ODIG-AUD, building and nurturing a knowledge sharing culture, and promoting a sense of belonging in ODIG-AUD. Additionally, improved communications flow needs to exist throughout ODIG-AUD, especially to the younger employees. Ways to make this improvement possible, besides a formal mentoring program, include having "open" meetings (such as strategy meetings, weekly team leads meetings, etc.) in order to keep everyone (especially the younger employees) better informed, and capturing and posting the minutes/summaries of these key meetings on the intranet.

▪ Develop an external approach to knowledge management to share knowledge with ODIG-AUD's customers and stakeholders. ODIG-AUD should concentrate on developing online communities of practice (similar to the World Bank's thematic groups) in order to encourage informal knowledge sharing among ODIG-AUD's staff, customers, and stakeholders. Online communities have been a very successful knowledge management strategy that many organizations are using (Fannie Mae Foundation, Best Buy, Hallmark, Federal Aviation Administration, NASA, Defense Acquisition University, Computer Sciences Corporation, etc.). ODIG-AUD should pilot a few online communities, with assigned facilitators/moderators, and see how things progress.

If ODIG-AUD incorporates all these recommendations toward developing its knowledge management strategy and implementation plan, it will be on its way to successfully applying knowledge sharing activities for transforming ODIG-AUD into a "learning organization" and improving communications and effectiveness internally and externally.

As part of the knowledge management strategy, various performance measures and metrics should be included. In studying the literature and analyzing ODIG-AUD, the following performance measures and metrics are proposed for the KM initiatives:

Measure: Improve customer readiness by enhancing knowledge sharing through collaboration and coordination.
> *Metric*: *Collaboration*—Actively posting documents, work notes, and discussion threads as part of an audit team's online community of practice (CoP) during the audit engagement to improve information and knowledge sharing for reducing time to produce audit report.
> *Metric*: *Mentoring*—Applying mentoring to help coach the audit team for improved team effectiveness.

Measure: Reduce "reinventing the wheel" by learning from others.
> *Metric*: *Lessons learned contribution*—Number of lessons learned (LL) entered into the LL repository after each major phase of an audit engagement.

Metric: *LL value added*—Demonstrating value-added benefits to review panels of what the knowledge recipient learned from accessing LL in LL repository.

Metric: *After-action reviews*—Conducting after-action reviews right after completing the audit and sharing this knowledge with others.

Measure: Build a better institutional memory through improved knowledge retention activities.

Metric: Personalization knowledge capture—Conduct knowledge sharing forums (brown-bag "lunch and learn" sessions, etc.), and apply organizational storytelling, and webcast these sessions.

Metric: Graybeards—Create an AUDIT Retiree and Alumni Association to share successes and failures (e.g., write case studies and share with current employees).

Metric: Codification knowledge capture—Codify knowledge captured through such items as compendium CDs (e.g., deskbooks, such as making the transition from a GS-13 to GS-14 Program Manager).

Measure: Create a stronger sense of belonging and community for instilling trust.

Metric: Knowledge sharing proficiencies—Achieving learning and knowledge sharing proficiencies as part of the annual employee performance reviews. Possible knowledge sharing proficiencies are shown in Table 2.1.

Table 2.1 Knowledge Sharing Proficiencies/Competencies

•	Communicates well with those within his/her department (intradepartmental communications).
•	Communicates effectively with those in other departments (interdepartmental communications).
•	Shares knowledge through various knowledge management mechanisms, such as mentoring, conference trip report discussions via brown-bag lunches, storytelling (organizational narratives), lessons learned/best practice content contribution, online communities/threaded discussions, newsletter contributions, etc. (knowledge contribution).
•	Actively participates in cross-functional teams (collaboration).
•	Regularly distributes articles of interest to other ODIG-AUD employees (knowledge dissemination).
•	Shows value-added benefits from knowledge received from others and knowledge gained by others (knowledge value).
•	Willing to be innovative, take risks, and try new ideas (knowledge creation).

Through the use of the knowledge audit survey, we also identified critical at-risk knowledge areas which may be at loss as shown below:

- ODIG-AUD's "institutional memory" and historical knowledge base
- Documented decision rationale
- Written instructions on doing routine tasks
- Relationship knowledge (i.e., who to go to for various types of questions)
- Audit skills and techniques
- Knowledge of the DoD (Department of Defense) organization

These types of critical at-risk knowledge seem to be pervasive in terms of other organizations experiencing the same pangs. Liebowitz conducted a knowledge audit/knowledge retention study and found the critical at-risk knowledge areas for another government organization as: administration knowledge, networking contacts, planning and monitoring, cross-functional knowledge, institutional knowledge, knowledge of information reporting, knowledge of multiple quality initiatives, and Section 508 (compliance for persons with disabilities) requirements for electronic files.

A key part of this potential knowledge loss is not only capturing an individual's corpus of knowledge but also capturing the individual's social network in order to know who to go to for certain types of questions and knowledge. Knowing the contacts and organizations to reach out to for answering certain questions is an important part of an individual's knowledge base. This type of knowledge cannot be replaced easily, because these "networks and relationships" have been built over time. It may be difficult for someone else to then apply these same networks because these social networks have been built on establishing trust between the individuals.

Another common type of knowledge that is often critical, but not retained, is the rationale on how decisions are made. Documenting the problem context, environment, issues, alternatives, criteria, and analysis in reaching a particular decision can be extremely useful when faced with a similar decision to make down the road. By capturing the decision rationale (pros and cons), the decision maker can apply or adapt his/her decision-making process for the target problem based on the historical examples. Learning from the past can be very insightful to help the decision maker in thoughtfully analyzing the new situation. Organizations need to do a better job of capturing this critical at-risk knowledge.

Looking toward the future, the UNESCO (United Nations Educational, Scientific, and Cultural Organization) held a summit in June 2007 titled "UNESCO High Level Group of Visionaries on Knowledge Acquisition and Sharing." They anticipate that, over the next 25 years, "learning will play an ever more active role in knowledge acquisition and sharing, including content creation and dissemination" [http://www.unesco.org]. Learning affects knowledge retention strategies by how well people are able to assimilate and comprehend other people's knowledge based upon their own learning styles. In the APQC's (American Productivity & Quality

Center) 2002 report on "Retaining Valuable Knowledge," 89% of the partners had discussions with senior management and interviews with employees or subject matter experts to determine what knowledge was critical to capture. Identifying this critical knowledge and relating it to learning behaviors will determine how successful organizations will be in applying their knowledge retention strategies in the future.

Chapter 3

Easy-to-Accomplish Knowledge Retention Techniques

3.1 Interviews

First-hand knowledge, or primary research techniques, can be gathered through the use of interviews. The interviews should be semistructured, where specific scenarios, questions, or topics would be prepared in advance, but would allow for adaptability in order to maximize the information content of the interviews.

The interviews could be structured among the themes of decision making, specifically strategic and tactical decisions made in the organization. Capturing the decision rationale of how decisions were reached and explaining the various factors and pros and cons of the alternatives are often overlooked in building an organization's knowledge base. A decision rationale template, similar to Figure 3.1, could be used as a framework in which to capture and structure the key points as related to the strategic and tactical decision making processes. Key learning templates, as shown in Figure 3.2, could also be used in conjunction with the decision rationale template. The knowledge elicitation sessions should use scenario building and organizational narratives as primary methods in which the tacit knowledge of soon-to-be retirees would be captured.

Decision/Assessment: _____

Prior Knowledge (What prior knowledge did you use as related to this decision making process?)	Factors/Criteria (What criteria did you use as part of your decision making process?)	Alternatives/Strategies (What alternatives/strategies did you use?)	Pros/Cons (What were the pros and cons of each alternative/strategy?)	What made the decision difficult?	Did You Make the Right Decision? If yes, explain. If no, then what should have been done differently?

Figure 3.1   Decision Rationale Template

Lesson Info:
- Lesson Number:
- Lesson Date:
- Submitting Organization:
- Submitted by:
- Contact Information:

Lesson learned title:

Abstract (2 to 3 sentences):

Description of driving event:

Lesson(s) learned:

Recommendation(s):

Documents related to lesson:

Knowledge area(s) [please check all appropriate]:

Impact, influence, or leverage of the lesson learned:

Approval Info:
- Approval date:
- Approval name:
- Approval organization:

Figure 3.2   Possible Template for a Key Learning Document

The interview protocol should be:

- Interviews will be scheduled in advance, and will last no longer than 2 hours.
- Preliminary questions tailored for the interviewee will be prepared for the interview and will be sent to the interviewee in advance for better content and time usage during the actual interview.
- The interviews will be audio-recorded, with permission of the interviewee, and will be transcribed for better understandability (an alternative knowledge capture process may be videotaping the sessions if allowed by the interviewee).
- The interviews will be semistructured with scenarios, questions, or topics prepared in advance, but will also be flexible to allow the interviewees to discuss their stories as related to their decision making-process.

The aforementioned templates will be used to better represent the knowledge being conveyed by the interviewer and to ensure that the uniformity of the interview process is preserved. Various interviewing techniques may be applied. Certainly, semistructured interviews should be used, along with the possibility of protocol analysis. Protocol analysis is a verbal walkthrough as the interviewee discusses aloud how he/she might solve a problem, respond to a scenario, or the like. Observation as a technique could also be applied to see how the users and providers are engaged in their work. Various "pushing the envelope" types of questions should be asked to stimulate some creative thinking, such as asking, "What would you have done differently if faced with the same situation?" or "Given the necessary time, if you could pursue up to five things that you wanted to do while on the job, what would those have been?" Focus groups could be used in order to get a better feeling for group decision making on projects.

3.2 Mentoring

Formal mentoring programs are popular techniques for knowledge retention, sharing, and transfer. Table 3.1 shows the description and call for mentors for NASA Goddard Space Flight Center's mentoring program.

Table 3.1   NASA Goddard Space Flight Center: Mentoring Program for 2007

The Goddard Mentoring Program is looking for mentors for the 2007 program. This program depends on the work of dedicated mentors for its success.
The purpose of the program is to provide an opportunity for all Goddard employees to benefit from developing a mentoring relationship or adding structure to an existing one. The program:

•	Creates opportunities for frequent and open interaction between employees at different organizational levels
•	Provides relationship-building activities to share organizational knowledge
•	Serves as a vehicle for transferring technical as well as formal and informal organizational knowledge

Mentors have the opportunity to share their knowledge, experience, and insight into how to get things accomplished, give back to the organization, build trust through increased communication, and be recognized as one of Goddard's outstanding mentors. Most importantly, mentors have the opportunity to see the impact of their efforts on the professional and personal growth of their mentees.
The Goddard Mentoring Program is a 1-year program that begins with an orientation session for all mentors, mentees, and mentees' supervisors. Early in the program, the systematic matching of mentors and mentees begins. All participants sign a mentoring agreement, which serves as the official commitment of time and effort for the mentor, mentee, and mentee's supervisor. Also, mentors will assist mentees with their Mentoring Action Plans that will outline the mentees' goals and the actions they need to take to achieve these goals. These plans will also include at least one developmental assignment and networking opportunity. Throughout the course of the program there will be regular meetings with mentors and mentees, formal mentor training, quarterly mentoring forums (brown bag lunch sessions), and opportunities to assess the entire program. At the end of the year, there will be a formal recognition ceremony in which each mentor and mentee who actively participated in the program will graduate and receive recognition.

Source: [http://ohcm.gsfc.nasa.gov/DevGuide/DevPrograms/Mentor/CallMen-tors2007.doc].

At Johns Hopkins University, a formal mentoring program exists as described below.

3.2.1 The Mentoring Program at Johns Hopkins University (JHU)

Mentee Training Program

[http://hrnt.jhu.edu/cmp/menteeTraining.cfm?SMSESSION=NO]

The JHU Career Information and Mentoring Network includes opportunities to learn from mentors in information interviews, career programs, shadowing, tutorials (2 months) and facilitated, long-term relationships (6 months).

Prospective mentees must submit an application, obtain supervisory permission, be selected for, and complete the Mentee Training Program. In this course, mentees will clarify their career goals and their objectives for participating in either a tutorial (skill building relationship) or long-term relationship (technical and interpersonal skill development, career exploration, networking, and learning about the Hopkins culture).

Mentees will gain knowledge about their learning and personality styles and how this information can be effectively applied in their mentoring relationship. Prospective mentees will leave the course knowing how to effectively establish mentoring agreements, complete a mentoring action plan, and take responsibility for managing their mentoring relationship.

Many fields have been using mentoring for years—medicine, law, trades, and the like. Learning from others, while on the job or in a simulated environment, is an excellent way to transfer knowledge. This contributes to knowledge retention, as it is a mechanism for passing knowledge on from one person to another.

3.3 Oral Histories, Storytelling

Besides mentoring, another approach to knowledge retention is through oral histories. Oral histories are a form of interviews and are basically stories or narratives that describe various episodes as conveyed by the speakers. They are a form of storytelling or organizational narratives. In Judith Moyer's 1993 book titled *Step-by-Step Guide to Oral History*, she describes an oral history as "the systematic collection of living people's testimony about their own experiences." Sandia National Labs, for example, has several thousands of hours of oral histories encoded as part of their knowledge preservation project. NASA developed the Oral History Project to capture knowledge from former astronauts about their space expeditions to the moon. An Oral History Association even exists (since 1966) and is dedicated to promoting people interested in oral histories [http://alpha.dickinson.edu/oha/].

Oral histories provide a wonderful mechanism for building the institutional memory of the organization. Capturing the knowledge of "graybeards" before they retire, or explaining the experiences of others while working in the organization can enhance the organization's historical knowledge base. Even though you do not have to do things "the way we have always done them in the past," it is informative to know how and why things were done a certain way. This knowledge can then be used to adapt other approaches to fit the new target situation.

An example of a quick 2-minute oral history is shown below:

Avoiding Being a Political Football
[http://pbma.nasa.gov]

I'm Jay Liebowitz, the Knowledge Management Officer at NASA Goddard, and I have a story about avoiding being the political football, and hopefully, you'll enjoy this. I was involved with a project where there were two teams of individuals who, it turned out, were doing the same, exact work. And I didn't realize that that was going to happen until I was doing my data collection effort and discovered that there was simply another team who was tasked to do the exact work that I was. I started to probe and wondered why that would be so, being a duplication of effort and resources. And it turned out, the management felt that the other team didn't have credibility because they lacked the technical subject matter expertise that was needed to conduct the study. However, I didn't have the domain knowledge which was necessary for properly carrying on the study. So, instead of trying to fight against the other team and be caught in the middle of this political football field, I decided to join forces with the other team, and it worked out extremely well. They were able to get the technical expertise necessary to do the work; I was able to get the complementary domain knowledge to carry out the work, and the bottom line was that the study that we both produced had very good reviews, and the management decided to follow those recommendations, and everyone was a winner. So, that was a nice way of trying to avoid being caught in the middle.

This type of occurrence could happen at any time, but it's probably most likely to happen in the formulation stage. So as you're putting together the teams and looking at various talents, you always want to make sure you have a complementary set of skills and also be very careful of some of the political nature of how people interact and the organizational dynamics. So, I think it's really critical—especially at the beginning stages—and hopefully, these types of activities will be useful throughout the project development phase.

Jay Liebowitz
Knowledge Management Officer
NASA Goddard Space Flight Center (GSFC)

3.4 Cheat Sheets

Most employees have their own "cheat sheets," which are notes, templates, short-cuts, simple heuristics that quickly allow them to accomplish some organizational task or process. These cheat sheets are quick reference aids which facilitate the owner's memory in getting things done. Ideally, these "memory aids" should appear on the organization's intranet, so others in the organization can benefit from them as well. They can be part of a continuity book.

These cheat sheets are ways to retain or capture knowledge in a codified manner. Whether they are simple mnemonics like "HOMES" for remembering the five Great Lakes in the United States (Huron, Ontario, Michigan, Erie, and Superior), or whether they are step-by-step procedures for accomplishing a process, these aids can be of great value to the organization. Typically, they are in the desk of a particular employee, but if made available to others, the broader organizational community could also derive great value.

3.5 Exit Interviews

Many organizations will conduct exit interviews before the employee leaves. Exit interviews can provide a snapshot of knowledge, but the research shows that many organizations try to capture the employee's knowledge within 90 days of their leaving and have been largely unsuccessful at doing this. Instead, a knowledge retention program should be planned out in advance whereby the employee's knowledge is captured at least 2 to 3 years before they retire. Ideally, a formal knowledge retention program should be planned from the first day of the employee's arrival through the last, as employees may quit the organization or leave early well before retirement age. By capturing knowledge during the employee's tenure, instead of a mad rush at the end, a greater likelihood for success exists in terms of retaining knowledge at different stages of the employee's career. Questions that the employee had early in his/her career may not even be remembered at later stages; thus, the ongoing capture of knowledge from day one may be useful to others instead of waiting until the end.

Much of the knowledge to be captured is not only in the individual's technical knowledge base but also in the employee's social network of relationships. When an individual leaves the organization, you are also losing his/her relationship knowledge in terms of who to go to for different questions in the organization and the social bond that exists between the employee and these individuals. Some people call this the "informal" organization, versus the formal organization chart. The grapevine effect is very strong in most organizations, and part of the exit interviews should be in identifying these social and organizational networks.

3.6 The Bible

Many organizations prefer to write "the bibles," if you will, in terms of capturing knowledge in various areas. DaimlerChrysler has the Engineering Book of Knowledge (EBOK) that is essentially the bible on the engineering aspects of their automobiles. It is a database containing their engineering best practices contributed by more than 5000 people and is divided into 3800 chapters. NASA has the NPG 7120.5D—the NASA Program and Project Management Processes and Requirements. It governs the formulation, approval, implementation, and evaluation of all NASA Agency programs and projects.

Writing the do's and don'ts of various organizational processes, as they relate to the core competencies of the organization, can be a very valuable aid. For example, Liebowitz developed an expert system to help people understand international business protocol. Here is a sample rule from the system:

IF you are doing business in Japan
AND you are interested in exchanging gifts
THEN
1. There are two times when business gifts are obligatory: July 15 and January 1.
2. Business gifts are frequently given at first meetings, but do not embarrass your Japanese counterpart by being the only one to show up with a gift.
3. Unless you have something for everyone present, give your gift while the recipient is alone.
4. Do not expect him to open the gift in front of you.
5. You should give and receive the gift with both hands and a slight bow [1].

Imagine a series of rules that deal with international business protocol in terms of doing business throughout the world. These could form the knowledge base as a "protocol bible" in how to negotiate business deals abroad.

3.7 After-Action Reviews

As mentioned in previous chapters, after-action reviews (AARs) could provide just-in-time knowledge retention. Knowing what went right, what went wrong, and how to fix things to be sure that things do not go wrong again comprise an after-action review. The military has been engaged in AARs for years, and industry, the government, and not-for-profits are applying the same techniques for knowledge capture, sharing, and transfer. USAID (The United States Agency for International Development) has produced a handy guide for conducting AARs [http://pdf.dec. org/pdf_docs/PNADF360.pdf]. According to the USAID [http://www.usaid.gov/ km/aar.htm], an AAR:

- Is a dynamic, candid, professional discussion of an event/task which focuses on the results of the event/task.
- Identifies the means to sustain what was done well as well as recommendations on how to improve shortfalls.
- Requires everyone's participation as these insights, observations, or questions will help the team identify and correct deficiencies or maintain strengths.

AARs are examples of lessons learned. They help provide reflective practitioners in terms of better understanding why events succeeded or failed. They can be a useful mechanism for knowledge retention and transfer. An example of an AAR observation worksheet used in the military is [http://www.au.af.mil/au/awc/awc-gate/army/tc_25-20/chap3.html]:

Training/exercise title:
Event:
Date/time:
Location of observation:
Observation (player/trainer action):
Discussion (tied to task and standard if possible):
Conclusions:
Recommendations (indicate how the unit could have executed the task(s) better or describe training the unit will need to improve future performances):
NOTE: Units may modify this format to meet their specific needs.
Another example of an AAR, and its benefits, is shown below [http://www. cibit.com/site-en.nsf/p/Vision-Knowledge_Management-Reflective_practice_in_ Knowledge_Management]:

For instance, in August 2003 there was a massive failure in the electricity distribution system in the USA. It had a significant impact on the Internet as primary and secondary servers lost their service and Web sites across the world became unavailable.

DTE Energy, the parent company of Detroit Edison, had introduced a program of informal, but structured learning, and staff were considering how they might respond more effectively in any similar future situations even while working to restore power to over 50 million USA and Canadian citizens. Within 24 hours DTE was able to convene a meeting where it could examine the AAR Observations of key staff members. Those AARs were combined into a collective lesson learned that will enable the company to plan for major training program for such large-scale emergencies in the future.

3.8 Online Communities, Wikis, Blogs, Social Networking Sites

Online communities, wikis, and blogs are popular personalization approaches for capturing, sharing, and disseminating knowledge. Online communities of practice or communities of interest allow people to post and share their insights on a particular topic of interest. Wikis and blogs also serve as mechanisms to share thoughts and ideas while capturing knowledge. Social networking sites, such as Facebook, MySpace, Friendster, LinkedIn, and others, also serve as vehicles to capture and share knowledge through the individual's social networks established through these sites.

With the exception of Wikis and online communities of practice, the user of the knowledge must be careful, as the knowledge may not always be correct. Blogs and social networking sites typically offer opinions of individuals, but this knowledge may not be either vetted for accuracy or validated through scientific means. Thus, the knowledge that is captured and transferred, at times, may not be the "gold standard" and could convey some erroneous information.

In spite of these possible limitations, we have moved into the "knowledge expression" era, where even avatars and artificial worlds take on the persona of individuals. We will continue to see the "connection" piece of knowledge management play a strong role to complement the "collection" side.

Reference

Axtell, R. (1993), *Do's and Taboos of International Protocol*, New York: John Wiley.

Chapter 4

Developing a Knowledge Retention Framework

In the "Knowledge Management Barometer Study," conducted in 2007 by the Federal German Ministry of Economics and Technology, a key conclusion was that knowledge management would continue to be a highly relevant topic over the next few years in Germany, Hong Kong, Denmark, France, the United States, Great Britain, and other countries. Part of the reason for this trend is the relationship of knowledge management (KM) to succession planning. KM should lead to workforce development and succession planning. According to the November 2006 Aberdeen Group Report, 73% of the companies surveyed have a plan or have budgeted to start one within a year; however, 27% still didn't have a succession plan. Thus, room exists for knowledge management to contribute to succession planning.

Knowledge retention is an important part of knowledge management. According to Daniel Alpert at the University of Oklahoma, knowledge retention strategies improve innovation, organizational growth, efficiency, employee development, and competitive advantage. At the UNESCO meeting on High Level Group of Visionaries on Knowledge Acquisition and Sharing, which met in June 2007, they stressed the need for improved knowledge acquisition models and strategies. Complementing their findings, Joe and Yoong [1] point out the importance of harnessing the expert knowledge of older workers. They indicate that there must be organizational readiness in retaining knowledge and skills. In addition, as discovered from the APQC "Retaining Valuable Knowledge" study [2], measuring the effectiveness of knowledge transfer is a major challenge to the design and implementation of knowledge retention initiatives. Part of this effectiveness might be measured through the social networks that are formed and the innovative ideas resulting from these networks. However, as cited in the Katzenbach Partner's 2007 publication, "The Informal Organization," the informal organization (the social or organizational networks) is "poorly understood, poorly managed, and often disregarded as inconsequential in most corporate settings [3]."

But, there is hope. The U.S. Census Bureau study in 2007 has indicated that more people are putting off their retirement or at least expect to work after retirement. According to Mbuya [4], the Pew Research Center report found that 77% of workers expect to work after retirement. This indicates that the experienced older workers will still be in the workforce and could help mentor others as part of their job. In industry, formal phased retirement programs exist whereby a retiree-eligible spends part of his/her time in the remaining months or years in mentoring their successors.

Let us now take a look at developing a framework for knowledge retention so that organizations can apply a model for accomplishing this task.

4.1　The Pillars of Knowledge Retention

There are four key pillars of knowledge retention. These are: (1) recognition and reward structure: making it a part of everyday life; (2) bidirectional knowledge flow: learning from your elders and from your juniors; (3) personalization and codification: looking at the connections and collections; and (4) the Golden Gem: bringing back the golden talent. Each of these pillars will be discussed in turn.

4.1.1　Recognition and Reward Structure

Everyone is busy and usually has a full plate of activities at work. Then, in order to be successful at knowledge retention (KR) activities in the organization, these KR activities must be embedded within the daily working lives of the employees, and people must be recognized and rewarded for accomplishing these KR functions. People generally like to be recognized and/or rewarded for their actions. Intrinsic motivators are typically more lasting and permanent than the use of extrinsic motivators. People want to feel good about themselves and their contribution to the organization. They want to be recognized in some manner, whether it is giving kudos to people at staff meetings, writing in the company's e-newsletter what they have done by mentoring others, or simply saying "thank you" when you see them in the hallway. Others, though, want to be rewarded for their actions, and some organizations are tying knowledge sharing activities to the employee's annual performance review. Pay-for-performance systems are also being established to include learning and knowledge sharing proficiencies.

Probably, to get the most value out of knowledge retention, both recognition and reward structures should be established. The reward does not necessarily have to equate to money. Giving a "Best Mentor" Award or a "Significant Learning" Award (for sharing one's bittersweet stories with others in the organization so that the knowledge recipient gains value by not going down the wrong paths) may be useful ways to show that someone's knowledge retention and sharing effort is valued by the organization. Some companies will not promote someone until they have either reached a certain level of knowledge sharing proficiency or have trained their successor. Whatever is the "secret formula" that works for the organization in motivating people to engage in KR activities should be discovered and applied.

4.1.2 Bidirectional Knowledge Flow

The second pillar of knowledge retention is bidirectional knowledge flow. This refers to the flow of knowledge from bottom up and top down. This has two connotations. Senior employees can pass knowledge down to junior employees, but also junior employees can transfer some of their specific knowledge to senior employees. Certainly, senior employees have many years of experience and have accumulated a wealth of knowledge over their working lives. Their knowledge should be retained and transferred to others in the organization. At the same time, the junior employees may have specialized skills and knowledge (technology area, new team-building approaches, new paradigm shifts in dealing with cross-generational knowledge flows, etc.) that also need to be retained and transferred to those in the organization. This two-way capture and flow of knowledge will help ensure the viability and longevity of the organization in terms of instilling a continuous learning culture. Typical questions to ask of the interviewed employees for knowledge retention purposes are:

1. What are the top ten questions people ask in your area? What documents and persons would be able to best address the answer to each question?
2. Please list and discuss the main business processes used in your area. Then, kindly give some helpful hints/tips/lessons learned, based on your experience, in terms of navigating through each of these processes.
3. What is the most difficult decision you had to make in your current position? How did you reason through this process?
4. With your years of experience behind you, what would you do differently if you were someone starting out in your organization?
5. What are the top five lessons you have learned that would enable you to be better prepared in your current position?
6. Talk aloud as you step through a typical scenario that involves an everyday type of decision that you need to make. This may be a reasoning process that takes 15 minutes or so to describe.

7. If I told you that you now have 5 minutes to reason through the process, please talk aloud about what you would do.
8. If you were developing a succession plan for your department, what are the critical components that you feel should be covered?

This capture and transfer process can be applied through personalization and codification approaches, which is the next pillar.

4.1.3   Personalization and Codification

The third important pillar in the KR framework is personalization and codification. Personalization emphasizes the "connection" part of knowledge management, and codification focuses on the "collection" or systems component. Capturing and transferring knowledge can be applied through both these approaches. In an organization, both personalization and codification should be used, and perhaps one of these two general categories will take dominance, based upon the organizational culture.

Examples of personalization approaches for knowledge retention and transfer include mentoring, job shadowing, job rotation, knowledge fairs, brown-bag lunches, storytelling, communities of practice, and other ways to facilitate connections between people. Certainly, expertise locator systems, online communities, and the use of social/organizational network analysis enable people to make connections.

Codification approaches are usually systems oriented, such as the use of lessons learned/best practice systems, after-action reviews, knowledge repositories on the intranet, multimedia asset management systems to capture webcasts and videos, and other systems-oriented approaches. Codification approaches help transform tacit knowledge into explicit knowledge so that it can be easily shared. However, personalization techniques can also make this claim, as storytelling is a prime example of how knowledge has been retained and shared over eons.

4.1.4   The Golden Gem

The fourth pillar of the KR framework is the Golden Gem, bringing back talented retirees into the organization. Some organizations are accomplishing this goal by hiring them as contractors or consultants, having a retiree and alumni association, having a ready pool of retired experts to use for projects, and other techniques. Some organizations are using formal phased retirement programs to help capture and transfer knowledge as someone is nearing retirement. Table 4.1 shows some possible ways to bridge the knowledge and skills gaps by bringing retirees into the organization.

Table 4.1 Programs for Involving Retirees

Phased retirement: Retirement-age employees continue in their old jobs but with scaled-down hours, typically 20 to 29 hours per week.
Retiree job bank: Allows retired employees to work up to a certain number of hours each year without adversely affecting their pensions.
Emeritus program: As a retiree, you still keep an office and e-mail address at your organization so you can come in periodically.
Part-time retired annuitant/project team consultant: Be part of a project team on a limited basis to share your expertise with the team in solving a specific problem.
Mentoring program: Serve as a mentor in a formal mentoring program in your organization.
Knowledge sharing forums: As an experienced individual, you would meet in a small group, once a month, of up-and-coming individuals to have you share stories, lessons learned, and insights.
Rehearsal retirement/boomerang job: An employee retires for a few months or a year, and then bounces back to the organization with limited hours.
Job sharing: More than one person sharing a job
Facilitator of an online community of practice: Act as a moderator of an online community in your area of expertise.
Knowledge capture/retention program: Be interviewed via video, and the video nuggets would be accessible over the Web in your organization.

4.2 Examples: Getting Started in Knowledge Retention

Some organizations are just getting involved with a knowledge retention program, partly due to the realization that the potential brain-drain effect is coming due to retirements. Below is an example of a statement of work issued from a government agency to help them further develop their knowledge retention program:

Statement of Work

Task Title: Knowledge Management: Information Collection and Retention
Statement of Work: Contractor shall complete the following tasks:

  A. Begin researching and developing preliminary draft outlining frameworks and protocols for conducting after-action reviews for critical lessons learned, best practices, communities of practice, and critical decisions derived from major projects/activities.
    1. Researching will include identifying and evaluating a product as a pilot for establishing a series of pilots for the purpose of documenting and publishing the results.

    2. The preliminary draft will outline how to capture information for the purposes of modifying Government University courses, best practices, and lessons learned.

    3. Conduct pilot programs.

B. Continue ongoing process of preparing and conducting interviews of additional twelve retiring employees based on KM model by focusing on positions with no established backups.

C. Produce a report for each interviewee documenting results of the interview.

D. Begin preliminary first steps to developing, drafting, and designing a taxonomy and knowledge map to begin organizing the information captured during the pilot and phase one of the KM project. This will be utilized as prototype for building a permanent repository.

E. Continue to conduct additional benchmarking by visiting other agencies established in knowledge management programs to identify best practices and recommendations for building the Knowledge Retention program.

Deliverables:

■ Provide a list of potential benchmarking sites to conduct a review and analysis of their processes and after-action reviews for knowledge retention.

■ Interview reports.

■ Preliminary draft for outlining strategy for capturing, collecting, transferring, and retaining information in modifying Government University courses, best practices, and lessons learned.

■ Preliminary draft outlining and developing Government Taxonomy and Knowledge Map.

■ Preliminary draft outlining framework and protocol for after-action reviews, including conducting several pilot programs to determine the appropriate framework.

■ Final Interview reports.

Another organization, the Servicewide Policy, Directives and Electronic Research (SPDER) organization at the Internal Revenue Service in Washington, D.C., wrote an "Expertise Retention Study of Strategic Human Resources (SHR)" in June 2003 and recommended the guidelines to perform and document a general knowledge analysis and specific item focus, as shown in Table 4.2.

To complement these guidelines, a knowledge access and sharing inventory might be used as part of the knowledge audit and knowledge retention study to identify key resources, relationships, and knowledge sharing practices. Figure 4.1 shows a possible knowledge audit instrument to use in an organization.

Table 4.2 Guidelines to Perform and Document a General Knowledge Analysis

Step	Description	Purpose
• Review organization's existing KM tools.	• Perform a knowledge audit. Research Web sites to identify explicit knowledge already captured, communities of practice already established, and any other existing venues such as shared drives, document management procedures, minutes. • Identify knowledge that should be and is integrated into the intranet.	• Educate and prepare the intern to design an action plan and fruitful questions. Interview questions should focus on identifying critical tacit knowledge at risk of being lost rather than what is already made explicit (e.g., Web sites).
• Review organization and SPDER project plan with sponsor.	• Discuss and have approved by the sponsor the plan of action. Adjust it accordingly. • Determine key players who will identify critical knowledge at risk and employees.	• Gain senior management endorsement. • Determine critical tacit knowledge at risk and identify who possesses it.
• Identify critical knowledge at risk and subject matter experts.	• Request senior management identify critical knowledge at risk and who possesses it. Include management and subject matter experts. Provide a by-name list of all employees, highlighting retirement eligible employees.	• Capture senior management ideas. • Determine critical tacit knowledge at risk, and identify who possesses it. These are your interviewees.
• Draft interview questions.	• Draft and tailor interview questions to the appropriate person, for example the chief human resource officer, a director, manager, or subject matter expert. They will identify critical knowledge at risk, those who possess it and existing systemic/procedural venues for capturing it. Some may not respond to terms such as tacit knowledge or communities of practice. Some may be interested in learning. Provide definitions and explanations. Adapt accordingly.	• Keep interview as short as possible by knowing what to ask to each person. • Educate interviewees on KM language in a manner to which he/she responds. Solicit responses on already established KM practices and tacit knowledge worth capturing.

Table 4.2 Guidelines to Perform and Document a General Knowledge Analysis (Continued)

Step	Description	Purpose
• Convert tacit critical knowledge to explicit and disseminate.	• Conduct interviews. • Identify tacit knowledge at risk and document results to include analysis on interview information. Perform second interviews if needed. • Provide summary of findings, recommendations, and next steps.	• Convert tacit critical knowledge to explicit and disseminate.
• Brief senior management and key players.	• Brief the organization's formal Community of Practice on findings and next steps to include critical knowledge not being captured and ways to do so.	• Bring awareness to the organization of KM tools being used. • Identify to managers opportunities to improve management of knowledge. • Develop the next steps.
• Disseminate results.	• (Optional) Implement formal communication plan on Web site. Post detail study purpose and results. Design links to SPDER and SHR.	• Share critical tacit knowledge at risk. • Share project results. • Increase awareness of KM.
• Provide final results to SPDER and the organization for decision/action.	• Provide managers results and corroborate future implementation plans. Assist decision makers with assigning future responsibility for gathering tacit knowledge.	• Establish future actions/milestones to implement capture and reuse of critical knowledge at risk. • Identify office and persons of responsibility.
• Measure performance.	• Perform periodic reviews 6, 12, and 18 months later checking on progress and implementation of recommendations to add upon existing venues.	• Determine effectiveness of study. Evaluate program performance to institute IM practices.

Figure 4.1   Knowledge Access and Sharing Survey (Developed by Dr. Jay Liebowitz, JHU)

A key part of developing a knowledge management strategy is to find out how people gain access to and share knowledge throughout the organization. This survey seeks to gather fairly detailed information about the ways in which you access, share, and use knowledge resources in your work. In answering the questions below, please keep in mind the following: answer for yourself, not how you think someone else in your job might answer; answer for how you *actually* work now, not how you wish you worked or think you should work.

We expect that some questions will require you to think carefully about the nature of the tasks you perform and how you interact with people both inside and outside the organization day to day. Carefully completing this survey will probably take about 25 minutes. *We appreciate your effort in helping us meet a strategic goal designed to make the organization more effective and to make it easier for all of us to do our jobs on a daily basis.*

Please forward your completed survey to _____ via e-mail _____ by ____. Thank you!

Please provide the following information:

Name: _____

Which department are you a part of: _____

How long have you been a full-time employee in the organization?

- ❏ Less than 6 months
- ❏ 6 months—less than 1 year
- ❏ 1 year—less than 3 years
- ❏ 3 years—less than 5 years
- ❏ More than 5 years

Please begin the survey!

In the course of doing your job, which resource do you most often turn to *first* when looking for information? (*please check only one*)

- ❏ E-mail or talk to a colleague in the organization
- ❏ E-mail or talk to a colleague who works outside the organization
- ❏ Do a global Web search (for example, Google, Yahoo)
- ❏ Go to a known Web site
- ❏ Search online organization resources (for example, intranet)
- ❏ Search through documents/publications in your office

❑ Post a message on a Listserv/online community to which you belong
❑ Ask your manager for guidance based on his/her experience
❑ Other *(please specify)* _____

What would be your second course of action from the above list?

_____

Think about the times when you have been really frustrated by not having a critical piece of knowledge or information you needed to get something done at the organization. Give an example, including the nature of the challenge and how the need eventually was met.

_____
_____
_____
_____
_____

Knowledge Resources

How often, on average, do you use each of the following to do your job?

	Daily	Weekly	Monthly	Quarterly	Never
Organization-wide database	❑	❑	❑	❑	❑
Organization-operated Web site (e.g., intranet)	❑	❑	❑	❑	❑
Department- or division-operated database (e.g., shared calendar)	❑	❑	❑	❑	❑
My own database or contact list file	❑	❑	❑	❑	❑
Organization policy/procedures manual or guidelines	❑	❑	❑	❑	❑
Department- or division-specific procedures manual or guidelines	❑	❑	❑	❑	❑
Vendor-provided procedures manual or guidelines	❑	❑	❑	❑	❑
My own notes or procedures	❑	❑	❑	❑	❑

List up to five resources (hard copy or Web-based) that you use to perform your job and indicate how often you use them. These resources can be journals, magazines, newsletters, books, Web sites, and so forth.

	Daily	Weekly	Monthly	Quarterly
1.	❑	❑	❑	❑
2.	❑	❑	❑	❑
3.	❑	❑	❑	❑
4.	❑	❑	❑	❑
5.	❑	❑	❑	❑

How often, on average, do you ask each of the following staff for help with understanding or clarifying how you are to perform your job, solving a problem, getting an answer to a question from a customer, or learning how to accomplish a new task?

	Daily	Weekly	Monthly	Quarterly	Never
Your immediate supervisor	❑	❑	❑	❑	❑
Your department head	❑	❑	❑	❑	❑
Your division head	❑	❑	❑	❑	❑
Subject-matter expert (in an area of policy, practice, or research)	❑	❑	❑	❑	❑
Technical or functional expert (e.g., accounting, legal, contracts administration, technology)	❑	❑	❑	❑	❑
A peer or colleague in your department or division (informal)	❑	❑	❑	❑	❑
A peer or colleague outside your department or division (informal)	❑	❑	❑	❑	❑

Name the top three people, in order, to whom you go when you have questions or seek advice in the following areas:

	One	Two	Three
General advice			
Management and leadership knowledge/advice			
Subject matter expertise/content knowledge			
Institutional/historical knowledge about the foundation			
Technical/procedural knowledge			

List up to five experts *outside* the organization whom you access to do your job. For each one, please indicate how often, on average, you contact them.

		Daily	Weekly	Monthly	Quarterly
1.		❑	❑	❑	❑
2.		❑	❑	❑	❑
3.		❑	❑	❑	❑
4.		❑	❑	❑	❑
5.		❑	❑	❑	❑

Knowledge Use

Which of the following do you *usually* use and/or perform (that is, on a daily or weekly basis) in doing your job? *(check all that apply)*

❑ Data or information from a known source (e.g., database, files) you have to retrieve to answer a specific question.
❑ Data or information you have to gather yourself from multiple sources and analyze and/or synthesize to answer a specific question.
❑ Instruction (step by step) you provide (that is, not a document) to a customer, vendor, or staff person.

❑ Direction you provide to a customer, vendor, or staff person (such as advice, counsel, or guidance, not step by step).

❑ Judgments or recommendations you are asked to make based on data or information that is given to you.

❑ Judgments or recommendations you are asked to make based on data or information that you must find yourself.

❑ Routine procedure or process for handling information, paperwork, requests, payments, invoices, and so forth (always done the same way).

❑ Variable procedure or process for handling information, paperwork, requests, payments, invoices, and so forth (requires some analysis and judgment to select the proper procedure or process to follow).

❑ Reports, memoranda, letters, or informational materials for customers, vendors, or staff that you must compile and/or write.

❑ Educational or promotional materials that you must compile and/or write.

❑ Proposals you develop to recommend new programs, projects, procedures, or processes.

After you have received, gathered, or produced information, instructions, documents, proposals, etc., and completed the task, what do you do with them? (*check all that apply*)

❑ Save them in an electronic file in my personal directory.
❑ Save them in an electronic file in a shared directory (e.g., p:drive, intranet).
❑ Save them in a personal paper file.
❑ Save them in a secure departmental paper file.
❑ Save them in an open departmental paper file.
❑ Share them or distribute them to others.
❑ Delete or toss them.
❑ Other *(please specify)*. _____

Sharing

When you come across a news item, article, magazine, book, Web site, announcement for a meeting or course, or some other information that may be useful to other organization staff, what are you *most likely* to do? (*check only one*)

❑ Tell them about it or distribute a copy to them personally.
❑ Post an announcement on the intranet.
❑ Send a broadcast e-mail.
❑ Send a memo or a copy through the interoffice mail.
❑ Intend to share it but usually too busy to follow-through.
❑ Include it in the Weekly Update.

❑ Ignore it.
❑ Other *(please specify).* _____

What are the constraints you face in being able to access or share knowledge?

_____
_____
_____
_____

What critical knowledge is at risk of being lost in your department or division because of turnover and lack of back-up expertise?

_____
_____
_____
_____

Training/Tools

When you want to learn or improve a skill or task, what do you prefer to do? (*check all that apply*)

❑ Get formal face-to-face training or course work outside the workplace.
❑ Get formal self-directed training (e.g., workbook, CD-ROM, online course).
❑ Have a specialist train me on-site.
❑ Train myself (informally, using a manual or tutorial program).
❑ Have my supervisor show me how to do it.
❑ Have a friend or colleague show me how to do it.
❑ Other *(please specify).* _____

What kind of tools or resources do you prefer to help you do your job? (*check all that apply*)

❑ Person I can talk to in real time
❑ Help line or help desk via phone, fax, or e-mail
❑ Advice via online communities of practice (on the intranet, Listservs, or other sources)
❑ Printed documents (for example, resource books, manuals)
❑ Electronic documents
❑ Audiovisual/multimedia material
❑ Special software
❑ Web-based utility, directory, or service
❑ Other *(please specify)* _____

Knowledge Needs

What information or knowledge that *you* do not currently have would you like to have to do your job better? Consider all aspects of your job, including administrative tasks, policies and procedures, interpersonal relationships, and so forth.

_____

_____

_____

What information or knowledge that *the organization* currently does not have do you think it should or will need to have to execute its mission, improve organizational effectiveness, and serve its customers with excellence? (You may answer for specific departments as well as for the organization as a whole.)

_____

_____

_____

To what extent do you agree with the following statements:

	Strongly Disagree	Disagree	No Opinion	Agree	Strongly Agree
I would benefit from having access to documents that contain introductory knowledge that I currently have to acquire from experts directly.	❏	❏	❏	❏	❏
I would benefit from templates to help me more easily capture knowledge (e.g., standard format for documenting what I learned at a conference or meeting).	❏	❏	❏	❏	❏
I would benefit from processes to help me contribute knowledge that I do not currently document or share.	❏	❏	❏	❏	❏
I would benefit from support to determine the most relevant knowledge to share for various audiences and how best to share it.	❏	❏	❏	❏	❏
I have knowledge in areas that I know the organization could benefit from but no way to make it available.	❏	❏	❏	❏	❏

Knowledge Flow

Imagine that you have just won the first organization Knowledge Sharing Award. This award is given to a person who shares his or her mission- or operation-critical knowledge so that the organization can be more effective. List the top five categories of knowledge that earned you this award and the category of staff with whom you shared it.

	Knowledge Category	Staff Category
1.		
2.		
3.		
4.		
5.		

How can the knowledge flow in your area of responsibility be improved?

_____

_____

_____

Additional Comments

Thank you for taking the time to complete this survey.

_____

_____

_____

References

1. Joe, C. and P. Yoong (2006), "Harnessing the Expert Knowledge of Older Workers: Issues and Challenges," *Journal of Information Knowledge Management,* Vol. 5, No. 1, World Scientific Publishing.
2. APQC (2002), "Retaining Valuable Knowledge," American Productivity & Quality Center, Houston, TX.
3. Katzenbach Partners (2007), "The Informal Organization," New York, NY.
4. Mbuya, J. (2007), "First Loves and Second Careers," *The Washington Post,* September 12.

Chapter 5

Knowledge Retention: Learning from Others

5.1 A Short Case Study: The Knowledge Retention Program for the Office of the Deputy Inspector General for Auditing (ODIG-AUD)

Based on the ODIG-AUD strategic plan, the ODIG-AUD knowledge audit, and the Knowledge Management (KM) Council-supported Knowledge Management Boot Camps, a great need exists to formulate a knowledge retention program for ODIG-AUD. With the number of retiree-eligibles steadily increasing at ODIG-AUD, the critical tacit knowledge gained over the years from these individuals should be captured, shared, and leveraged throughout the organization and to the stakeholders. As a result, the knowledge retention program will be comprised of three parts: people, process, and technology.

5.1.1 People

The ODIG-AUD knowledge audit preliminarily identified individuals at ODIG-AUD who possess key knowledge critical to the future strategic success of ODIG-AUD's mission. These individuals were cited by others as the "go-to" person for certain types of knowledge—whether subject matter domain expertise, strategic knowledge, process knowledge, institutional/historical knowledge, or relationship (who knows who) knowledge. These individuals were also cited because they were nearing retirement age, no backup expert exists, and their critical "at-risk" knowledge was strategic to ODIG-AUD's mission.

These individuals from the knowledge audit serve merely as a starting point to capture their knowledge before they leave the organization. A more comprehensive knowledge inventory of those possessing ODIG-AUD critical at-risk (could be lost) knowledge needs to be conducted by types of knowledge important to ODIG-AUD's future success. A listing needs to be compiled through either the use of social network analysis (to identify key sources of knowledge that people go to in ODIG-AUD) or through allowing management to identify key people out of the retiree-eligible list. Thus, Step 1 is to identify the critical at-risk knowledge areas and corresponding experts through either a full-scale social network analysis of ODIG-AUD or simply start with the preliminary list of individuals from the knowledge audit coupled with management's list of people to interview out of the retiree-eligible list.

Once the list of people who possess the critical at-risk knowledge is assembled, the individuals can be prioritized based on when they are eligible to retire, their availability, and other criteria.

5.1.2 Process

After identifying the key sources of knowledge, Step 2 is to develop a process for knowledge capture. This process should not be conducted simply 90 days before a person retires. Rather, the academic studies show that planning 2 to 3 years ahead will greatly improve knowledge capture efforts.

One important part of the knowledge capture process is the use of lessons learned and organizational narratives. After-action reviews (AARs) may already be used within ODIG-AUD to determine lessons learned and best practices. For example, after each audit engagement, the AAR may consist of three questions:

1. What went right and why?
2. What went wrong and why?
3. How can we ensure we do not make the same mistakes?

The AAR should be conducted during the middle and end phases of the audit engagement with each audit team.

Organizational narratives, or "storytelling," should also be used by the individuals to be interviewed and collectively by the audit project team. A trained facilitator should be utilized to conduct the interviewing sessions, which should last no longer than 2 hours per session. The interviewing sessions should be videotaped, so they could later be edited and included in a Web-based, online searchable video repository (called a multimedia asset management system). Software for searching on queries in the video repository is available through Convera and Virage.

The various councils at ODIG-AUD are another rich source of knowledge. Best practice templates, cheat sheets, and personal contact files should also be captured and included as part of the overarching knowledge retention program. These should be housed on the ODIG-AUD intranet.

Last, various knowledge retention roles and responsibilities will need to be included for specific ODIG-AUD staff. Being a knowledge steward, knowledge retention manager on projects, and the like will facilitate the knowledge retention program. Learning and knowledge sharing proficiencies should also be part of National Security Personnel System (NSPS) to encourage a knowledge sharing culture.

5.1.3 Technology

KM-related technology should be an enabler to the knowledge retention process. The last step is to invest in technology to support the knowledge retention program. We previously highlighted the continued use and expansion of the ODIG-AUD intranet, as well as updating and enlarging the existing expertise locator system. The new multimedia asset management system will need to be created to store, retrieve, and search on the knowledge acquisition interview videotapes. Again, the use of Convera or Virage could be used as a search engine and archive. There may be a need for software like Autonomy to help organize the knowledge and build a knowledge taxonomy for operations and maintenance.

5.1.4 Summary

The knowledge retention program at ODIG-AUD involves three steps:

1. People: Identify key individuals whose knowledge assets need to be retained.
2. Process: Apply knowledge capture processes as previously discussed.
3. Technology: Invest in technology to support the knowledge retention efforts.

These three steps, along with proper succession planning and workforce development, will ensure that ODIG-AUD will continue to thrive in the coming years, long after the current generation retires. The sooner ODIG-AUD embarks on this knowledge retention program, the better ODIG-AUD will become.

5.2 Best Practices of the Private Sector and Universities for Using Retirees as a Form of Knowledge Retention and Transfer

Retiree-work programs have been used by a number of companies. Travelers Insurance's program for rehiring retirees, Tray Temps, allows Travelers to have its own job bank of retirees to fill temporary work needs. Travelers has found that hiring a retiree is more productive than hiring a new or temporary worker, as there is no learning curve. Honeywell has also hired retirees on a part-time basis for positions for which they have expertise or skill gained through tenure. Eastman Kodak has a similar program for hiring retired workers [4]. Some companies put retiree's names on banners hung in prominent places to give them recognition.

Booz Allen and Hamilton, an international consulting firm, has a knowledge retention program in place via their Knowledge On Line system. Booz Allen has a policy of paying team members to spend a week or two after a project is finished entering what they have learned into its Knowledge On Line system in order to not reinvent the wheel for future projects [5].

In terms of companies utilizing and supporting older workers, Wells Fargo has had success with manager training sessions that address generational differences. ChevronTexaco piloted a program with Ceridian where an elder care professional is sent to the home of an employee's family member to assess the person's needs and make a recommendation [6]. Eastbay is another company interested in recruiting older workers. There are about 150 people over the age of 50 who work for the company's 450-employee call center [7]. Manufacturers like WireMaid Manufacturing Ltd. and Weather Shield Manufacturing Inc. are making efforts to attract and retain workers older than 55. A major concern among these manufacturing companies is not having enough trained workers as older workers retire. In fact, a survey in the Milwaukee area 5 years ago found that 60% of manufacturing workers in that area planned to retire within 10 years. Manufacturers are trying to create more flexible work schedules and add benefits and perks to keep the older workers at the companies. Weather Shield is also considering rehiring some retirees on a part-time basis, perhaps working a short week or 4-hour shifts [7]. Avaya, Monsanto, PepsiCo, and Lockheed Martin offer phased retirement to their employees. Monsanto has over 600 phased retirees, and the phased retirement was created to retain the best older workers and provide a flexible workforce [9].

MITRE Corporation enables older employees to stay in the workforce not only through phased retirement, part-time work, and sabbaticals, but also through its "Reserves at the Ready" program. This program allows employees with at least 10 years of company service to become part-time on-call employees staffing projects throughout the corporation [11]. Mentoring by the older workers has also been actively utilized through the Reserves program. Sears has a buddy system where an older employee is paired with a younger, entry-level employee [10].

Kmart Corp, Ford Motor Co., Xerox Corporation, and other companies are seeking out retired executives to help them regain their footing [1]. These former executives have "a lot of experience in the trenches" and "know how to manage in downturns" [1]. However, there are those who believe that the younger generation should be given a chance to take over. For example, Robert MacDonald, who retired as chief executive of Allianz Life of North America, said he doesn't think drawing top executives from the retirement pool is a good idea [1]. He believes it is a delaying tactic to avoid facing the issues you have for long-term leadership [1]. Some industry retirees are disgusted at the high salaries that current executives are making, while taking away pension and health care benefits from the retirees. For example, the 90,000-member Association of BellTel Retirees is one of many in a new, nationwide organizing effort made up of former white-collar managers and executives who are disgusted by corporate greed and outraged by pension and health-coverage take backs [2].

As a result of retirees reentering the workforce, a new concept of "unretirement" has begun to emerge. A study by Drake Beam Morin revealed that one in two people, regardless of age, find career transitions successful. According to Schultz [3], many companies are bringing back former employees as independent contractors. "Contingent workers" (independent contractors, returning retirees, consultants, and freelancers) are an increasing segment of the work force. The job of developing and implementing corporate culture programs is obviously trickier when a significant number of the workers are not employees of the corporation. A U.S. Department of Labor report notes that misclassification of nontraditional workers "is not an easy problem to solve, and will only get worse as more nontraditional workers join the labor force" [3].

In Government Accounting Office's (GAO's) human capital study [8] of nine private sector organizations, ten key human capital principles were distilled:

- Treat human capital management as being fundamental to strategic business management.
- Integrate human capital functional staff into management teams.
- Leverage the internal human capital function with external expertise.
- Hire, develop, and sustain leaders according to leadership characteristics identified as essential to achieving specific missions and goals.
- Communicate a shared vision that all employees, working as one team, can strive to accomplish.
- Hire, develop, and retain employees according to competencies.
- Use performance management systems, including pay and other meaningful incentives, to link performance to results.
- Support and reward teams to achieve high performance.
- Integrate employee input into the design and implementation of human capital policies and practices.
- Measure the effectiveness of human capital policies and practices.

Universities have also been active in involving their retired faculty. The Henry Koerner Center at Yale University involves retired professors in teaching, provides them with research money, offers computer help, and plans social activities. At the Retirement Center at the University of California at Berkeley, a "Learning in Retirement" program is taught by and for retired faculty and staff members. Retired professors at the University of Southern California can receive research stipends of up to $2000, and the Emeriti College holds an off-campus lecture program featuring retired professors [12].

5.3 Other Lessons Learned in Knowledge Retention

From Corning:

- Get a realistic time check. Understand how long it will really take to implement knowledge retention initiatives.
- Secure top management support.
- Ensure IT support and buy-in; ensure that the IT staff understands that this is not solely an IT initiative. Technology is certainly part of the process, but it shouldn't drive the process. Participation is what matters the most in KR.

From Northrop Grumman:

- People fundamentally want to share knowledge, but management systems get in the way.
- Top leadership championship is required.
- A burning issue is the ticket into knowledge management.
- After-the-fact tacit knowledge codification is almost futile; you need to facilitate people-to-people learning or tacit knowledge transfer.
- IT solutions are a necessary evil.
- People understand knowledge management with time.

From The World Bank:

- Both technology and corporate culture must be addressed.
- Design and serendipity need to be balanced.
- Both internal views and client perspectives are needed.
- Keep it simple.
- Anchor knowledge sharing activities in core business processes.
- Metrics are mandatory, so use proxies to demonstrate the value of knowledge sharing and retention on the front line.
- Develop and maintain the permanent capacity to facilitate the brokering of knowledge (via thematic groups and advisory services or help desks).

From Xerox Connect:

- The necessity of a disciplined approach and proven methodology.
- The need for clear and regular communications regarding the status of the organization (e.g., where it was and where it is going) and why it mattered.
- The need for communication across and up the organization.
- The participation and buy-in of a diverse group of people.
- Knowledge is an evolution, not a revolution.
- KR and Management is a continuous process that needs to watched day to day.
- Leverage what already exists for knowledge retention, sharing, and management.
- The initiative must support the business, or it will not work.
- Measure continuous improvements.
- You can derive great benefits from having the different initiatives work together.
- Focus on value creation (e.g., innovation).
- Give people the ability to ramp up. You cannot ensure your people will have a job, but you can ensure they have employability.

From Tennessee Valley Authority:

- Knowledge loss through attrition: Strategic lessons learned
  - There is a logical process.
  - Focus on critical positions—one job at a time.
  - Lots of detailed work, analysis, planning, and project management.
  - Limited number of ways to deal with it.
  - Everyone must do their part—management, HR, supervisors, process owners, KM professionals.
- Knowledge loss through attrition: Tactical lessons learned
  - Clarify purpose to employees and defuse concerns.
  - Include newer employees as "observers."
  - "How did you learn it?" enlightening.
  - Clusters of knowledge based on career path.
  - Safety and reliability/risk drive priorities.
  - Retirees can be a continuing resource.
- Knowledge loss through attrition: Suspected lessons learned
  - Less at-risk knowledge than suspected.
  - Risk greatest in technical/operational positions and in problem solving strategies.
  - "Big brain" systems seldom the answer.
  - Redesign/reengineering opportunities emerge.

 – Process can drive establishment of communities of interest, technology, and other responses.

5.4 Learning from Others about Lessons Learned Systems and Processes

5.4.1 What Works and What Does Not

Lessons learned systems have been used in the military, industry, and government for many years. In the military context, they are a natural extension of the after-action review (AAR) process in understanding what worked, what did not, and how best to ensure something will work in the future. Celebrating the successes, but also explaining the failures and bittersweet stories, is part of weaving the organizational fabric in terms of building a continuous learning culture [15].

In APQC's "Retaining Valuable Knowledge" study [13], they found that after-action reviews were typically used by Siemens and Xerox in order to leverage and share lessons learned. Gartner, in their "Key Issues for Knowledge Management 2007" [16] report, and Liebowitz [17] indicate that the use of social networking software will continue to become pervasive as a way for sharing knowledge. The Fraunhofer Institute in College Park, Maryland, has been developing the Software Experience Factory over the years in order to apply lessons learned to software engineering. Andrade et al. [18] have also encouraged the software engineering community to develop a lessons learned system for critical software. And the Department of Energy, through their Society for Effective Lessons Learned Sharing (SELLS) [http://hss.energy.gov/CSA/Analysis/ll/sells/], has been actively involved in the lessons learned process of their energy-related activities for more than 10 years. They created the DOE Corporate Lessons Learned Program Standard (DOE-STD-75-1-99) to formally explain their lessons learned program and related assessment guide.

Unfortunately, there have been many stumbling blocks to effectively develop and institutionalize lessons learned systems and processes. According to Thomas Cowles of Raytheon, the following are typical responses from users and managers in terms of using lessons learned systems and processes [http://www.dtic.mil/ndia/2004cmmi/CMMIT2Tue/LessonsLearnedtc3.pdf]:

■ "It's a pain to weed through all the irrelevant lessons to get to the few 'jewels.' There should be an easier way to find the lessons that pertain to me."
■ "Many of the lessons just seemed to repeat a company practice or instruction. Who thought this was a 'lesson learned'?"
■ "It takes almost two weeks to review the lessons in the database. Who's got the time for that?"
■ "We seem to learn some lessons over and over again."

- "Until we can adopt a culture that admits frankly to what really worked and didn't work, I find many of these tools to be suspect."
- "Despite the processes and procedures in place to capture and share lessons learned, I see no evidence that lessons are being applied toward future success."

These comments echo a number of concerns when developing lessons learned systems and processes.

First, the lessons learned processes must be embedded into the daily work activities of the employees; otherwise, people will not have the time and incentive to use these lessons learned processes and systems due to their already full plate. NASA, as part of their NASA Program and Project Management Guideline NPG 7120.5, requires NASA project teams to capture and apply lessons learned throughout the project development life cycle. These lessons learned can be captured and accessed through the NASA Lessons Learned Information Systems/NASA Engineering Network or other lessons learned repositories used by the project teams. During project team reviews, the review chairs can question the project managers about their use of lessons learned, and the project managers need to be prepared to respond to their inquiries. An interesting comment from Dr. Ed Hoffman, Director of NASA's Academy for Program/Project Engineering Leadership, during the author's conversation with him in summer 2007 indicated that the lessons learned systems in the NASA environment were not as effective as the personalization approaches used at NASA. At the Jet Propulsion Lab, a legacy session "personalization" approach is used to learn from project experiences. This involves a work session where team members identify innovations and improvements they have made during their project that have potential value to future users [19]. Thus, each organization should apply both codification and personalization approaches to mitigate risks.

A second observation about lessons learned systems is that many of them are ineffective due to passive analysis and dissemination of the lessons. Weber and Aha's work [20] showed that the just-in-time delivery of military lessons learned significantly improved plan execution performance measures. In earlier work, Weber et al. [21] found that 70% of lessons learned systems are ineffective due to the passive analysis and dissemination of the lessons to users. To encourage a more push versus pull approach, lessons learned systems should "push out" appropriate lessons to potential users on a timely basis. One way of doing this is to have a user profiling feature or intelligent agent that will send an e-mail of the "new lesson" URL to potential users when new lessons are entered into the lessons learned system that fit the user's interest profile. Lessons learned systems (like NASA's Lessons Learned Information System (LLIS)—llis.nasa.gov) help in capturing, analyzing, and disseminating appropriate lessons to enable project teams and organizations strive for success. For example, NASA's Lessons Learned Information System includes over 1800 lessons in project management, safety, systems engineering, and other areas that benefit the NASA community. Additionally, instead of relying on a "pull" approach for disseminating lessons, a "push" approach is used through user interest profiling. New lessons that fit the completed user's interest profile are sent via e-mail, with the appropriate URL links, to the user to immediately access the lesson. Even though most of the lessons learned systems are passive in their collection, analysis, and dissemination processes, future lessons learned systems would apply more active techniques via intelligent agent technology to dynamically create a user's interest profile and send relevant new lessons directly to the user [22,23].

A third potential obstacle to applying lessons learned systems and processes is that people are not rewarded or recognized for their efforts. The NSPS pay-for-performance system in the military and parts of the government may be a way to recognize and reward people for such efforts through their annual performance reviews. Johnson and Johnson, The World Bank, and other organizations include learning and knowledge sharing proficiencies as part of their employee annual performance review. Lockheed Martin also requires an individual to train his/her successor before the individual can be promoted. American Management Systems used to publish the *Best Knews* monthly newsletter that would highlight the individuals and their respective lessons that were used most often during a given month by others. Other organizations may have a "Significant Learning" award given to individuals or teams whose lessons created the most value as determined by their knowledge recipients. Recognition and reward systems are important components in order to further incentivize people to actively capture and use lessons learned systems and processes.

A final potential obstacle is validating what is truly a "lesson learned." When the author was the Knowledge Management Officer at NASA Goddard Space Flight Center, he was partly responsible for overseeing the operations, maintenance, and future development of the agency-wide NASA Lessons Learned Information System (LLIS). Part of this process was vetting "lessons learned." Each of the ten NASA Centers had different processes on how to accomplish this task. At NASA Goddard Space Flight Center, the lesson had to be approved through the individual's management chain before it could be sent to the LLIS team for further review. At the Jet Propulsion Lab, an expert review panel met every 2 to 4 weeks to review any new lessons in their respective area that were submitted for possible inclusion in the LLIS. In order for NASA to improve its lessons learning process, GAO issued a number of recommendations [24]:

- Articulate the relationship between lessons learning and KM through an implementation plan for KM.
- Develop ways to broaden and implement mentoring and storytelling as mechanisms for lessons learning.
- Identify incentives to encourage more collection and sharing of lessons among employees and teams, such as links to performance evaluations and awards.
- Track and report on the effectiveness of the agency's lessons learning efforts, using objective performance metrics.

- Designate a lessons learned manager to lead and coordinate all agency lessons learning efforts.
- Enhance LLIS by coding information and coding an easier search capability to allow users to identify relevant lessons, including more positive lessons, provide a means to disseminate key lessons to users, and solicit user input on an ongoing basis.
- Establish functional and technical linkages among the various center- and program-level lessons learning systems.

To become successful in applying lessons learned systems and processes, a knowledge sharing culture needs to be built and nurtured. Along these lines, Liebowitz [15] suggests some key "Knowledge Sharing Tenets for Success":

- Enhance reward and recognition system to include learning and knowledge sharing competencies.
- Acquaint people with knowledge sharing and its benefits.
- Share the message that with creativity comes failure, and we all benefit from talking about our successes and our failures.
- Integrate knowledge sharing into everyone's job.
- Educate people about what types of knowledge are valuable and how they can be used.
- Make sure the technology works for people, not vice versa.

In terms of lessons learned regarding knowledge management (KM) initiatives, the following may be useful:

- It is easier to apply KM strategies that fit an organization's culture than to first change the organizational culture and then apply KM.
- Do not try to do everything at once.
- Apply KM to the core competencies of the organization to show value-added benefits.
- There will always be skeptics of anything.
- Do not put the cart before the horse.
- About 80% of knowledge management is people, culture, and process, and 20% is technology.
- KM should lead to innovation, productivity, knowledge retention, people retention, and "mission success."
- Closely align your knowledge management strategy with your organization's business strategy.
- KM must be woven within everyone's daily work activities, as opposed to something else to do on top of one's full plate.

Taking these knowledge management, lessons learned obstacles, and knowledge sharing tenets into account, the lessons learned process should be a systemic one. That is, the capture, application, sharing, and generation of lessons learned should be woven within the organizational culture (or perhaps within the project development life cycle). Providing mechanisms for rating the value of a particular lesson, similar to Amazon.com, may promote the use of lessons learned throughout the organization. Providing other ways to recognize and reward people for contributing their lessons should be strongly considered, either through the annual employee performance review or otherwise. Additionally, having active analysis and dissemination of lessons for pushing appropriate lessons to targeted users may reduce the barrier of "looking at yet another system." Certainly, having a process for vetting lessons learned is also needed, as well as archiving outdated lessons.

5.4.2 Possible Lessons Learned: Proof of Concept Criteria

In order to show proof of feasibility of a lessons learned system or process, various measures or metrics could be used:

- Ability to quickly capture lessons learned into the system: this would be determined by the time difference between this new process versus the status quo.
- Ability to improve performance and decision making through our embedded lessons learned process: after-action reviews or retrospective learning would need to be conducted after decisions are made to determine whether informed decision making was created through our new process.
- Quality of the knowledge captured through our process: this would be determined by the knowledge recipients to determine the value-added benefit of the knowledge gained from the lessons learned process.
- Amount of knowledge captured through our process: the number of lessons learned or knowledge artifacts captured through our new process would be compared with those captured through the status quo. For example, the research indicates that interviewing is more effective than protocol analysis in terms of the knowledge facts gathered from the knowledge elicitation process.
- Ease of use in both incorporating lessons learned into the process, as well as in accessing the lessons learned: this would need to be determined by the expert and user evaluations of the process/system.
- Ease of the ability of the user to browse, search, and retrieve the lessons learned.
- Adaptability of the approach in terms of how generic is the methodology as applied to other domains: this would be evaluated by application of the approach to multiple domains.

- Ease of archival and maintenance of the lessons learned process: this would have to be compared with that of the status quo.
- Flexibility of the approach in terms of getting appropriate lessons learned to the user at the right time (based on the user's dynamic interest profile) and in terms of searchability of the lessons learned.
- Ability for the process to enable continuous learning to take place in terms of increasing the organizational intelligence.

References

1. Moses, A. (2002), "Companies in Trouble are Turning to Their Retirees," Associated Press, July 21, http://www.nctimes.net/news/2002/20020721/61048.html.
2. Conlin, M. (2002), "Revenge of the Retirees," *Business Week*, November 18, http://www.businessweek.com/magazine/content/02_46/b3808119.htm.
3. Schultz, A. (2001), "The IRS and the Independent Contractor Knowing the Rules of the Game," July, www.prounlimited.com/biofarm_the_irs.html.
4. Cyr, D. (1996), "Lost and found—retired employees," *Personnel Journal*, Vol. 75, No. 11, November.
5. Cone, E. (1998), "Managing the Churning Sensation," *Information Week*, May 4.
6. Bloomfield, J. (2003), "What's Changing in the World of Employers?" Alliance for Work-Life Progress newsletter, April, www.onesmallstep.org.
7. Gearhart, K. (2003), "Employers change their views of older workers," *Wausau Daily Herald*, January 26.
8. United States General Accounting Office (2000), "Human Capital: Managing Human Capital in the 21st Century," Testimony by David Walker, Comptroller General of the United States, GAO/T-GGD-00-77, March 9.
9. Walsh, M. (2001), "No time to put your feet up as retirement comes in stages," Global Action on Aging, www.globalaging.org, April 15.
10. Condenzio, L. (2003), "Best Practices in Recruiting and Retaining Employees," Harvard University, www.nacufs.org/resources.
11. Wellner, M. (2002), "Tapping a silver mine," *HR Magazine*, March.
12. Fogg, P. (2003), "Good and Gray," *The Chronicle of Higher Education*, August 15.
13. American Productivity and Quality Center (2002), Consortium Learning Forum Best Practice Report, "Retaining Valuable Knowledge: Proactive Strategies to Deal With a Shifting Work Force," Houston, TX.
14. Landon, J. (2002), A Briefing on Knowledge Retention: Capturing Knowledge Before It Walks Out the Door, TVA University, April.
15. Liebowitz, J. (2006), *What They Didn't Tell You About Knowledge Management*, Scarecrow Press/Rowman & Littlefield.
16. Mann, J. (2007), "Key Issues for Knowledge Management 2007," Gartner Research, February 12.
17. Liebowitz, J. (2007), *Social Networking: The Essence of Innovation*, Scarecrow Press/Rowman & Littlefield.

18. Andrade, J., J. Ares, R. Garcia, J. Pazos, S. Rodriguez, A. Rodriguez-Paton, and A. Silva (2007), "Towards a Lessons Learned System for Critical Software," *Reliability Engineering and System Safety*, Vol. 92, Elsevier.
19. Cooper, L, A. Majchrzak, and S. Faraj (2005), "Learning from Project Experiences Using a Legacy-based Approach," Proceedings of the 38th Hawaii International Conference on System Sciences, IEEE.
20. Weber, R. and D. Aha (2002), "Intelligent Delivery of Military Lessons Learned," *Decision Support Systems Journal*, Vol. 34, Elsevier.
21. Weber, R., D. Aha, and I. Becerra-Fernandez (2001), "Intelligent Lessons Learned Systems," *Expert Systems With Applications Journal*, Vol. 17, Elsevier.
22. Liebowitz, J. (2006), "Business Intelligence Cannot Exist Without Knowledge Management," http://www.businessintelligence.com/ex/asp/code.123/xe/article.htm.
23. Liebowitz, J. (2006), *Strategic Intelligence: Business Intelligence, Competitive Intelligence, and Knowledge Management*, Auerbach Publishing/Taylor & Francis.
24. Holm, J. (2002), "Lessons Learning and Knowledge Management," NASA KM Workshop, NASA JPL, January 30.
25. Pennington, G. (2007), "Lessons Learned About Knowledge Retention," Mantech Corporation, Lexington Park, MD.

Chapter 6

Calculating the Loss of Knowledge

Anecdotally, we might hear someone say that if Mary ever left the organization, we would be in trouble. There are many Marys in an organization, and this thought often permeates most of the organizations in existence. Mary might be the only person who knows some specialized knowledge important to the organization, or she might be the only person who knows the ins and outs of getting something done. Or even better, Mary's claim to fame is that she knows who to go to for getting your questions answered.

Certainly, if Mary were to leave the organization, there could be a major gap that would need to be filled. Of course, organizations should apply succession planning at all levels in the organization; however, we know that this usually is not done very well. So, how can we try to calculate the potential loss of knowledge if Mary or others were to leave the organization?

This chapter will explore some ideas along these lines in order to better assess the loss of knowledge in an organization.

6.1 The "Grayout" Factor

Knowledge loss will be apparent in many industries. According to Blake Melnick, the chief knowledge officer at Atlantis Systems Corporation, examples of pending grayout include [1]:

- 75% of aircraft technicians will be retiring between 2006 and 2010, based on a Canadian Forces study.
- 40% of the technical workforce of original 1970s reactors will retire between 2005 and 2010, based on an International Atomic Energy Agency Study.

Besides energy and aerospace, other industries including manufacturing and even education are witnessing similar issues with pending mass retirements. Federal, state, and local governments are also experiencing similar pangs in terms of the baby boomers retiring. So, is there a way to calculate this potential grayout loss?

One method as a crude measure to calculate potential knowledge loss is:

$$\Sigma((\text{number of people leaving in a given year}) (\text{measure of knowledge worth})$$
$$(\text{loaded salary})) - \Sigma((\text{number of replacements for those people in a given year})$$
$$(\text{measure of knowledge worth}) (\text{loaded salary}))$$

The measure of knowledge worth would be from 1 (low) to 10 (high) in terms of the individual's knowledge base as related to the strategic mission of the organization.

We can apply this formula to the following example. Assume that five people will be retiring this coming year, and three of those individuals will be replaced, we can calculate the net knowledge loss as shown in Table 6.1.

However, the fallacy with this approach is that perhaps there is just a net knowledge loss of $100K, because the company may only want to keep Joe, Mary, and Sherry because Alice and Mark don't contribute greatly, in terms of knowledge worth, to the strategic mission of the company. Since the knowledge worth values

Table 6.1 Sample Calculation of Net Knowledge Loss

People Leaving	Knowledge Worth	Loaded Salary	Total
Joe	8	$100K	$800K
Mary	10	$110K	$1100K
Alice	2	$50K	$100K
Mark	3	$70K	$210K
Sherry	9	$60K	$540K
			$2750K
Replacements	Knowledge Worth	Loaded Salary	Total
Kirk for Joe	7	$100K	$700K
Joan for Mary	10	$120K	$1200K
Jim for Sherry	9	$60K	$540K
			$2440K

Net Knowledge Loss = $2750K – $2440K = $310K.

for Mary's and Sherry's replacements (that is, Joan and Jim, respectively) are the same as those of Mary's and Sherry's, then the only difference may be that Joe's replacement (Kirk) has a knowledge worth value of 7 versus Joe's of 8. Given the same salary for Kirk as Joe's ($100K), then the knowledge loss may be only $100K (that is, $(8 - 7) \times \$100K$). If Kirk had a knowledge worth value of 9 or higher, then there would have been a knowledge gain (versus a knowledge loss).

A better approach may be a more methodical process of calculating return on investment as related to potential brain-drain effects. Knowledge Harvesting, Inc. [http://www.knowledgeharvesting.com] has developed a knowledge harvesting methodology in working with many clients over the years. As related to knowledge loss, they cite the brain-drain orientation as the "gradual depletion or complete loss of valuable knowledge that is essential to the success of the organization" [2]. In performing their knowledge harvesting ROI (return on investment) analysis, they use the following steps [2]:

1. Definition: Describe the situation; determine the orientation; review the project plan.
2. Cost analysis: Calculate cash outflows associated with labor; determine costs of maintenance labor; calculate cash outflows associated with plant, property, and equipment.
3. Benefit analysis: Determine noncash benefits; determine the nature of the benefit stream; select applicable performance measures.
4. Computation: Calculate cash inflows; determine the cost of capital; calculate net present value; assess impact to earnings before income tax, return on assets, free cash flow.

According to McManus et al. [2], the average cost of turnover is 1.5 times the annual salary of the job, and on average, it takes 13.5 months for new employees to reach their maximum efficiency. This could also be factored into the brain-drain calculations. From the work of McManus et al. [2], the ROI for a brain-drain orientation project is estimated at a ratio of 10:1. For a brain-drain project, 24 months is the estimated lifetime of the produced knowledge asset (until the time that some adaptation is warranted) [2].

Another interesting approach to calculate knowledge loss is to tie value to the business processes and decisions made by a given individual. Value network analysis could be used to assign value based on an individual's knowledge base and contacts, and how his/her knowledge affects the business processes and business decisions in the organization. This could then lead to a dollar value associated with the individual's impact on the bottom line of the organization. Value network analysis is a derivative of social/organizational network analysis, which will be explained in the next chapter.

Another method of calculating knowledge loss is to examine new business opportunities lost due to a perceived lack of talent from impending retirements and attrition. If key individuals in the organization leave, the prestige and "worth" of the organization may diminish. For example, if a football team loses their top quarterback and running back to free agency, then the effectiveness of the football team may be dramatically affected if equal replacements are not found. From the outside world's perception, the "worth" of the team may decrease due to the loss of these key players. Ticket holder sales may also decline due to the outside perception that the team will not be as good as before without these players. Similarly, new business opportunities (ticket sales in our football analogy) may be lost due to reduced credibility of the team players. Business opportunities lost can be determined by the proposal bids from possible contracts that were not awarded to the organization.

A last technique to determine knowledge loss is to simply calculate the individual's percentage share of revenues to the organization. By determining the role of the individual as a principal investigator/team lead/team member on contracts awarded to the organization, the dollar value of his/her participation can be computed based on his/her percentage share of the revenue dollars brought into the organization. Thus, if an individual is responsible for bringing in 25% of the revenues per year into the organization, based on the contracts awarded to the individual, then his/her dollar worth may be $5 million/year if the organization averages $20 million in revenues per year.

Thus far, we have been discussing only the dollar worth of an individual if he/she leaves the organization. But the intangible benefits may be greater than the tangible ones if someone leaves. The "knowledge" loss will be even greater due to the social networks that he/she has built over the years, as well as the potential loss of community building within the organization. For example, someone may be a wonderful colleague and mentor to others in the organization, as well as a great team builder. When the individual leaves the organization, there is a multiplicity factor as this individual touches the soul of many other individuals, both internal and external to the organization. Calculating a value for this internal and external "outreach" is difficult to determine. Perhaps the loss of certain customers could result by having someone leave the organization due to the personal bond that was established by the individual and the customer.

6.2 Turning Knowledge Loss into a Positive Gain

Most chief executives will tell you that their competitive edge is their people in their organization. You typically want to surround yourself with intelligent advisors so that your decision-making process will be better informed. It is similar to playing tennis with people who are slightly better than you so that your tennis game can improve. In much the same way as tennis, organizations derive power from their employees and the relationships that they build and nurture between their organization and their customers and stakeholders.

Losing people in the organization can impact the organization, but a knowledge loss could be a potential gain. How could this be so? First, if an organization needs to improve fiscally, a rightsizing/downsizing effort could result in cutting costs for the organization. Here, a deliberate attempt to let go of people may result in a gain by reducing costs to the organization. Second, many organizations are outsourcing their call centers and help desks to also reduce costs. In this case, people internal to the organization may also be asked to leave if they were involved in performing these duties. The organization hopes to achieve some positive gain by outsourcing. Last, some people who have been with the organization for many years may not be as innovative as others, as they might tend to view things as "the way we have always done it." In order to increase innovation in organizations, fresh ideas are needed, which could result in the hiring of new employees. Certainly, the knowledge loss of employees who retire from the organization could be offset by the knowledge gain by new employees who may generate creative ideas to spark new products and services for the organization.

In spite of these possible scenarios, some people are very hard to replace. Some managers, however, may feel that everyone can be replaced, but this may not necessarily be true. The combination of intelligence and experience by working many years in an organization can be a winning formula. Also, some people have a sixth sense and an intuitive feeling for how things should work. Getting this "gut feeling" can be difficult and often requires one's knowledge base built on experiential learning and facts. Certainly, today's environment is very data intensive, and we can use technology and advanced analytics to help make predictions and informed decisions. Coupling experience to data intelligence can be a powerful marriage, and organizations will have to find the right balance to capitalize on this synergy.

6.3   Knowledge Retention at Tennessee Valley Authority (TVA): Assessing Knowledge Loss

Since 1998, the Tennessee Valley Authority (the largest public power producer in the United States) has been very active in knowledge retention activities. Industry-wide, 21 energy companies reported that 90% of them indicate attrition as an important or emerging issue, yet only 30% of them have a plan to address this issue [3]. TVA was facing similar concerns with knowledge retention issues, as one-third of their workforce was eligible to retire in 5 years (as of March 2007) [4]. To specifically address the avoidance of knowledge loss through attrition, TVA applied several approaches [3]:

- Establish loss-prevention projects.
- Define loss-prevention plans and goals.
- Identify critical at-risk knowledge.
- Identify key individuals.
- Record and codify explicit knowledge.

- Transfer tacit knowledge through mentoring.
- Develop network-based access.
- Establish networks of designated experts.

TVA's main questions as related to the knowledge retention process were [3]:

1. Specifically, what knowledge is being lost?
2. What are the business consequences of losing each item of knowledge?
3. What can we do about each item?

In retaining critical knowledge, TVA applied the subprocesses of conducting a knowledge loss risk assessment, determining an approach to capture critical knowledge, and monitoring and evaluating. Knowledge loss risk assessment looked at two major factors: time until retirement and position criticality [4]. The retirement factor times the position risk factor equaled the total attrition factor. The outcome indicators are the number of positions/incumbents assessed, action plans implemented, and human performance errors related to knowledge [3]. The outputs were [3]: documentation of critical institutional knowledge, sufficient number of employees with critical knowledge, reengineered/eliminated/outsourced skills, training needs, mentoring opportunities, and rotational assignment opportunities. Examples of knowledge retention options used at TVA include identifying a coworker to cross-train, provide formal education and training, apply structured self-study and mentoring, and update/develop documentation and procedures [4].

To help the managers at TVA monitor and evaluate the knowledge retention plans, several key metrics are used, such as [4] headcount versus business plan; attrition and replacements; problem areas and actions planned; and knowledge retention status (high priority and position criticality). A key lesson learned from the TVA experience was that the risk was greatest at specialized technical positions and in problem-solving strategies [4].

6.4 Summary

Calculating the potential loss of knowledge in an organization is not a trivial exercise. This chapter provided some ideas on how to accomplish this task, but measuring the intangibles is never easy [5]. One of the difficulties involves determining the worth of one's network. The next chapter will take a look at social/organizational network analysis to help identify knowledge flows and knowledge gaps in organizations.

References

1. Melnick, B. (2007), "Managing 'Greyout' at Atlantis Systems," *KM Review*, Vol. 10, No. 2, Melcrum Publishing, May/June.
2. McManus, D., L. Wilson, D. Fredericksen, and C. Snyder (2004), "Business Value of Knowledge Management: Return on Investment of Knowledge Retention Projects," www.knowledgeharvesting.com.
3. Landon, J. (2002), "A Briefing on Knowledge Retention: Capturing Knowledge Before It Walks Out the Door," TVA University, Tennessee, April.
4. Wright, A. (2007), "Knowledge Retention: TVA's Approach to Retaining Critical Knowledge of an Aging Workforce," Northeast Public Power Association Conference, March 2, http://www.tva.gov/knowledgeretention/pdf/neppa_march07.pdf.
5. Liebowitz, J. (ed.) (2008), *Making Cents Out of Knowledge Management*, Scarecrow Press/Rowman & Littlefield.

References

1.

Chapter 7

Using Organizational Network Analysis to Inform Knowledge Retention Efforts

Many organizations are embarking on applying social or organizational network analysis in order to better understand the knowledge flows and knowledge gaps in their organization and to inform their knowledge retention strategy. Organizational network analysis (ONA) can identify these knowledge flows and "structural holes," as well as uncover certain types of brokering roles that individuals play in a given network. The central connector is the individual to whom people come often for advice. The liaison is the individual who spans between two groups. The peripheral specialist is the individual who is "outside" (on the periphery) of the network and is often isolated and unconnected from the network. Each of these brokering roles can be influential in the creation, sharing, transfer, and management of organizational knowledge.

The central connector can work in one's favor or not. For example, the central connector can be the "carrier" of information and knowledge to allow the knowledge flows to be fluid. Or on the contrary, the central connector could be a bottleneck if he/she desires. This would inhibit the knowledge sharing process. In generating strategic intelligence, a central connector could play an important role, as he/she is typically at the hub of the social network interactions and could greatly facilitate the development and dissemination of the strategic intelligence.

The liaison can be someone who links his/her group with another group in the organization, or an individual who links two groups separate from his/her own. This person may have a fair amount of relationship knowledge, knowing "who knows who," to help produce and disseminate strategic intelligence. This person is a "networker" who can build the tentacles of social links to quickly spread the word.

The peripheral specialist is either a newcomer to the organization or perhaps an expert in a particular field. The neophyte has not been able to develop his/her social network, as he/she is new to the organization. The expert may be a particular scientist or individual who can do his/her work without the need for interacting with many others. The IT (information technology) or computer guru may be this type of person. However, it becomes harder to find these peripheral specialists in organizations, because almost everyone has their own social network of one kind or another. Even if you have a well-known researcher in the R&D department of an organization, that individual cannot really work in isolation. They need to connect with marketing and sales so that they can better understand the customer's requirements in order to develop new products that the customer will want to buy, and the R&D folks need to let the sales and marketing departments know what new products are coming down the line, so they can be marketed appropriately. Thus, the peripheral specialist, even though somewhat isolated, still has a role to play toward contributing to strategic intelligence [1,2,3,4].

7.1 Case Example: The Department Organizational Network Analysis

7.1.1 Respondent Demographics

A Web-based survey was used to gather the information for the department ONA. There were seven respondents who completed the department ONA pilot. Three of them have been a member of the department for 16 years or more, one for 11 to 15 years, two for 7 to 10 years, and one for less than 1 year. The primary role or function of these individuals within the department program is: two individuals for program/project management, one for modeling modules management, one for fleet modules management, one software engineer, one support engineer, and one systems administrator. Three of the seven respondents are in the same work location. The other individuals each work in a separate location.

7.1.2 Insights Gained from the Department Organizational Network Analysis (ONA)

The Web-based survey asked questions dealing with whom the respondents contact internally and externally (at least once a week) regarding various types of knowledge associated with the department program. InFlow, a social/organizational network analysis tool by Valdis Krebs [http://www.orgnet.com], was used to help in the ONA.

In terms of seeking knowledge internally, at least once a week, for various types of knowledge, A is typically the go-to person, with B not far behind. For general knowledge regarding department modules and functionality, most people seek out A first and then B. B is a contractor who seems to be heavily relied on for many types of knowledge. For legacy or historical knowledge, most people seek out A first and then B close behind. The same holds true for configuration management knowledge questions and subject matter domain knowledge-related questions. A is, by far, the heaviest sought-out individual in the department team, and unfortunately he may be leaving within the next 2 years. He is also the first go-to person for strategic or leadership advice, contracts/budget questions, and questions relating to new ideas or challenging problems at work. C plays an influential role as a go-to person relating to questions dealing with new approaches, leadership/strategic knowledge, relationship knowledge, and questions dealing with challenging situations at work. For relationship knowledge ("who knows who" types of knowledge), D and A play the leading roles as the main point-of-contact. E, B, F, and G were cited by the survey respondents as people they contact for internal types of questions.

For seeking department customer requirements, problem-solving knowledge, and subject matter domain knowledge from external contacts, there was a fairly even distribution across all respondents; however, X Corporation was a key player. Certainly, X Corporation was highly sought out for contractor support questions dealing with department hardware and software. H, I, N, and J were respectively sought out as external contacts for contracts/budget-related questions. X Corporation and N were most sought out as external contacts for discussing a new or innovative idea. B, K, L, and a fleet contact were also cited as key external contacts for a challenging work situation, in addition to X Corporation and N.

In terms of brokering roles, A and B are central connectors. For most types of knowledge, they are typically sought out for their advice. A and D are frequently cited as liaisons, connecting between two groups. In fact, D had the highest value for relationship knowledge in terms of people seeking her out for knowing who to go to for certain types of knowledge. In terms of isolates or peripheral specialists, M may be in this role partially because she is so new to the department (being there less than 1 year).

In terms of different types of centrality, degrees are a measure of "activity" in terms of the number of direct connections for a node. A and B are certainly the go-to people in terms of their direct connections. Betweenness centrality is a measure of "control" which indicates how much a node controls the flows in the network based on its role in serving as an intermediary between other nodes. A and C typically have high betweenness values, indicating that they can be the facilitator or possibly the inhibitor to knowledge flows in the department. They both, along with D, have high power values as well. Closeness centrality is a measure of "access."

Typically, someone who is close to a key decision maker would have a high value for closeness centrality. In the organization chart, A and M have higher senior management positions relative to the other respondents. A typically reaches out to C for various types of internal knowledge. C has a higher closeness centrality value compared with the others. In terms of network reach, the department can easily get to different people on the department with one or two hops.

In performing cluster analysis on the department network, cliques and social circles can be computed. A clique is a group of nodes with direct connections to each other. A social circle is a group of nodes with direct or indirect connections to each other. In a social circle, all nodes can reach each other in a maximum of two steps. Because there is such a small network, most people on the department have either direct or indirect connections to each other. Certainly, A and C have a strong direct relationship with each other. Because of the "smallness" of the network, there really are not any "structural holes" in terms of information not typically passing through an individual or department.

In terms of tenure in the organization, most people on the department are fairly senior. M is the youngest member on the team (less than 1 year), in terms of tenure on the department. However, she has direct links to A and others who are senior members of the team.

7.1.3 Knowledge Retention Recommendations Based on the Department ONA

The department ONA was an excellent prototype to use as part of the knowledge retention effort, due to its relatively small network. From conducting the ONA, several key recommendations can be made:

- The importance of A's knowledge and social network should not be taken lightly. With A being eligible to retire in 2 years, a knowledge retention effort should commence focused on A's knowledge base.
- B, a contractor, is also a key player in terms of being sought out for different types of knowledge. The knowledge retention effort should also focus on B's knowledge and social network.
- M, being relatively new to the department yet in a senior management role, will ultimately form the direct connections to be a greater part of the department network. As M has direct links to A, a mentoring effort by A may get M more tied into the network structure.
- D and A have the strongest values for their "relationship knowledge." They seem to know best who to contact to get certain questions answered. Based on their relationship knowledge, a knowledge map might be developed and placed on the department intranet to link typical questions that are asked to people, documents, and business processes.

■ C, with his high betweenness and closeness centrality values, is also a key individual whose "liaison" knowledge should also be captured, perhaps as part of the knowledge map.
■ A general rule for promotion or merit pay increase might be similar to Lockheed Martin's policy for promotion. In order to be promoted for certain positions, one of the promotion criteria is that you must train/educate your successor (before you can be promoted).

7.2   An Example of an ONA Survey Instrument

In order to perform an organizational network analysis, a Web-based survey is typically used to collect the data. Follow-up interviews are then conducted as well to clarify some of the information collected through the surveys. An example of an ONA survey is shown in Figure 7.1. This particular survey, built on the work of Liebowitz, Rob Cross at the University of Virginia, and ManTech Corporation, is probably longer than most ONA surveys, but it will give the reader an idea of the type of questions that can be asked.

Figure 7.1   Program Network Assessment Questionnaire

You are being asked to complete the following Organizational Network Analysis Survey because you individually possess knowledge and information regarding the personnel network that makes your program a success. This survey and its questions are designed to highlight both the internal and external network of professionals that are in some way associated with providing the products and services to the user populations. Thank you in advance for completing this survey.

A. Basic Demographics
   1.   What is your full name:
   2.   How long have you been a member of the program team?
        Please choose only one of the following:
     a. Less than 1 year
     b. 1 to 3 years
     c. 4 to 6 years
     d. 7 to 10 years
     e. 11 to 15 years
     f. 16 years or more
   3.   What is your primary role or function within the program?
   4.   Where is your primary work location?

B. Program Team Characteristics

5. How well do you rate your team's ability to work together with other teams?

6. How well do you rate your team's agility in terms of being well suited to

(Weak)		(Neutral)		(Strong)
___	___	___	___	___

deal with uncertainty and unfamiliarity?

7. How well is there a shared understanding of command intent among your team?

8. How well do you rate your team's ability in terms of generating interactions between and among any and all team members?

9. How well is there situational leadership on your team whereby no single person will be in charge all the time?

10. How well would you rate your team as being nonhierarchical?

11. How well would you rate your team's degree of competency?

12. How well would you rate your team's ability as being a good multitasker?

13. How well do you rate your team's ability to utilize information technology via a robust network to facilitate information sharing?

14. How well does your team exhibit strong work values among your team?

15. How well does your team exhibit strong family values among your team?

16. How well does your team exhibit strong communications flow among your team?

17. How well does your team exhibit strong interpersonal trust among your team?

18. What is the degree of cultural issues affecting your team?

19. How well does your team encourage incentives to share knowledge?

20. How well does your team exhibit reciprocity of knowledge shared among your team?

21. How well does your team exhibit loyalty among your team members?

22. What is the degree of gender issues affecting the team?

23. What is the degree of cross-generational biases among the team?

C. Knowledge Characteristics and Contacts

24. How do you rank the knowledge types below as being most important to the team (1 = low and 6 = high):

_____ Relationship knowledge ("who knows who" knowledge)

_____ Strategic knowledge (management/leadership advice)

_____ Process knowledge

_____ Subject matter domain knowledge
_____ Historical/institutional knowledge
_____ General knowledge

25. Whom do you contact internally (at least once a week) for general knowledge regarding your program modules and functionality provided?
    Please write the names and organizations here:
    1st choice:
    2nd choice:

26. Whom do you contact internally (at least once a week) for relationship knowledge (seeking people who will know whom to contact to answer your questions) regarding your program modules and functionality provided?
    Please write the names and organizations here:
    1st choice:
    2nd choice:

27. Whom do you contact internally (at least once a week) for strategic knowledge (management/leadership advice) regarding your program modules and functionality provided?
    Please write the names and organizations here:
    1st choice:
    2nd choice:

28. Whom do you contact internally (at least once a week) for process (methodology) knowledge regarding your program modules and functionality provided?
    Please write the names and organizations here:
    1st choice:
    2nd choice:

29. Whom do you contact internally (at least once a week) for expert/subject matter domain knowledge regarding your program modules and functionality provided?
    Please write the names and organizations here:
    1st choice:
    2nd choice:

30. Whom do you contact internally (at least once a week) for historical/institutional knowledge regarding your program modules and functionality provided?
    Please write the names and organizations here:
    1st choice:
    2nd choice:

31. Whom do you contact externally (at least once a week) for general knowledge regarding your program modules and functionality provided?
    Please write the names and organizations here:
    1st choice:

2nd choice:

32. Whom do you contact externally (at least once a week) for relationship knowledge (seeking people who will know whom to contact to answer your questions) regarding your program modules and functionality provided?

    Please write the names and organizations here:
    1st choice:
    2nd choice:

33. Whom do you contact externally (at least once a week) for strategic knowledge (management/leadership advice) regarding your program modules and functionality provided?

    Please write the names and organizations here:
    1st choice:
    2nd choice:

34. Whom do you contact externally (at least once a week) for process (methodology) knowledge regarding your program modules and functionality provided?

    Please write the names and organizations here:
    1st choice:
    2nd choice:

35. Whom do you contact externally (at least once a week) for expert/subject matter domain knowledge regarding your program modules and functionality provided?

    Please write the names and organizations here:
    1st choice:
    2nd choice:

36. Whom do you contact externally (at least once a week) for historical/institutional knowledge regarding your program modules and functionality provided?

    Please write the names and organizations here:
    1st choice:
    2nd choice:

37. Whom do you typically turn to for help in thinking through a new or challenging problem at work (could be an internal or external contact)?

    Please write the names and organizations here:
    1st choice:
    2nd choice:

38. Whom are you likely to turn to in order to discuss a new or innovative idea (could be an internal or external contact)?

    Please write the names and organizations here:
    1st choice:
    2nd choice:

39. When you need information or advice, which person is generally accessible to you in a reasonable amount of time to solve your problem (could be an internal or external contact)?

    Please write the names and organizations here:

    1st choice:

    2nd choice:

40. Whom do you turn to for input prior to making an important decision (could be an internal or external contact)?

    Please write the names and organizations here:

    1st choice:

    2nd choice:

41. Whom do you often see in informal activities with you (could be an internal or external contact)?

    Please write the names and organizations here:

    1st choice:

    2nd choice:

42. Who has contributed the most to your professional growth and development (could be an internal or external contact)?

    Please write the names and organizations here:

    1st choice:

    2nd choice:

43. Whom do you turn to for personal support when your work is going poorly, a project is failing, or you are frustrated with certain decisions (could be an internal or external contact)?

    Please write the names and organizations here:

    1st choice:

    2nd choice:

44. Who gets you the most energized in your daily work (could be an internal or external contact)?

    Please write the names and organizations here:

    1st choice:

    2nd choice:

45. Whom do you trust the most to keep your best interests in mind (could be an internal or external contact)?

    Please write the names and organizations here:

    1st choice:

    2nd choice:

7.3 Knowledge Retention through the ONA Lens

ONA provides a lens in which an organization can view future knowledge retention issues. Key people who possess critical at-risk knowledge can be easily identified, and knowledge flows and gaps in the organization can be determined. Additionally, individuals who broker knowledge between groups can be identified, as well as those who sit on the periphery of the network. Capturing the knowledge and social network of those who broker connections can be a vital part of an organization's knowledge retention program. These people form the bridges to the islands of expertise in the organization, and their relationship knowledge should be important to preserve. Of course, the "who knows who" relationship knowledge is typically built on trust and years of working together. Thus, it may be difficult to simply retain one's social network when someone leaves or retires from the organization, because this type of knowledge has been built over time through the personalities of others. At the very least, a knowledge map can be developed whereby various types of questions can be linked to organizational units for gaining answers to those questions.

References

1. Liebowitz, J. (2006), *Strategic Intelligence: Business Intelligence, Competitive Intelligence, and Knowledge Management*, Auerbach Publishing/Taylor & Francis.
2. Liebowitz, J. (2007), *Social Networking: The Essence of Innovation*, Scarecrow Press/Rowman & Littlefield.
3. Liebowitz, J. (2006), *What They Didn't Tell You About Knowledge Management*, Scarecrow Press/Rowman & Littlefield.
4. Liebowitz, J. (2004), *Addressing the Human Capital Crisis in the Federal Government: A Knowledge Management Perspective*, Elsevier/Butterworth-Heinemann.

Chapter 8

Case Study: Knowledge Harvesting during the Big Crew Change

Jeffrey E. Stemke
Knowledge Strategist, Chevron Corporation

Larry Todd Wilson
Founder and President, Knowledge Harvesting Inc.

Many companies face a historical challenge in their workforce age demographics. As increasing numbers of senior employees edge closer to retirement, new employees are recruited to fill their places. The loss of experienced personnel combined with the influx of young employees is creating unprecedented knowledge retention and transfer problems that threaten companies' capabilities for operational excellence, growth, and innovation. We need to exploit practical, effective retention and transfer processes and tools to minimize business disruption and accelerate competency development.

A few years ago, in a discussion of critical issues facing the oil industry, Chevron's CEO Dave O'Reilly outlined the following goal for global talent management:

> We will no longer be talking about the big crew change. We will have taken the steps needed to ensure that a trained, global workforce and a pipeline of future leaders are in place.

In this chapter, we present a high-level description of how Chevron is turning talk into action, particularly highlighting a new tool in our knowledge retention arsenal: knowledge harvesting.

8.1   Business Case

The impending crew change was first brought to the attention of the oil industry more than 20 years ago. Our challenging business presents many possible career opportunities to motivated employees, and most individuals are satisfied pursuing a career within Chevron. The major source of attrition, therefore, is retirement rather than leaving to work for other companies. As a result, our hiring rate resembles a sine wave; we hire a large number of people every 20 to 30 years, they enjoy a rewarding career, and then we bring on the next crew.

So why are we, like many other industries, not better prepared for changing age demographics? One reason is the huge generation of baby boomers making way for the much smaller group of GenXers. In addition, the oil business has changed significantly in the last 20 years. Organizations downsized during the 1980s and 1990s as the economy slowed and technology increased personnel efficiency. This downsizing reduced our bench strength and limited the time available for mentoring by senior staff. The number of graduates with earth science and geophysics degrees dropped as other disciplines gained popularity. As a result, today's hiring cycle is vastly different from what current leaders and supervisors experienced when they were hired.

The following scenarios illustrate some increasingly common knowledge retention challenges:

■ Key experts will retire in the next few years, sometimes without skilled replacements ready to take over their responsibilities.
■ Critical knowledge and experience is at risk when experts transfer or retire, and there is insufficient time, staff, or budget to reinvent it.
■ Critical processes are difficult to document since they require considerable experience to run safely and efficiently.
■ A large number of newly hired employees need accelerated competency development.
■ Successors inherit cabinets full of files from people who have left the organization; however, the inheritors receive no explanation of their value and have little opportunity to rediscover their importance.

An experienced workforce is essential to delivering the organizational capability to operate and expand any business. However, the way we work has evolved, and we must account for this shift in our training and knowledge retention methods. Gone are the days when work could be portioned into individual assignments. Today, we rely on multidisciplinary project teams and integrated processes or supply chains to accomplish most of our results. Professionals and managers have a deep (but often narrow) knowledge of complex technical and political systems. They rely on relationships with colleagues for the knowledge necessary to accomplish their tasks.

Modern industry's wide distribution of expertise requires a more sophisticated approach to capturing, documenting, and sharing knowledge. If companies fail to address these new approaches to analysis and networking, knowledge drain will create significant business disruption.

8.2 The Learning Life Cycle

Knowledge and experience gained by an expert throughout his or her career is extremely intricate and difficult to distill. Therefore, retention efforts should not be exclusively focused on end-of-career events. Business divisions and corporate human resource or workforce development groups should collaborate in creating an employee learning life cycle that spans the entire career. Chevron informally connects many of such knowledge retention processes as part of employee learning and development.

New hires benefit greatly from on-boarding processes that introduce them to their work and help them begin to form their personal networks. Chevron has created early career-focused learning processes ("Horizons") in a number of disciplines such as earth science, petroleum engineering, and information technology. As part of the annual performance planning process, each employee develops a personal learning action plan directed toward specific competencies. Belonging to a community of practice (CoP) in your discipline is a good way to learn from colleagues to solve day-to-day problems or to tap into documented expertise such as best practices, tools, and career development roadmaps with relevant training resources. No matter what your discipline, the best way to learn is by doing—gaining experience through a series of project assignments.

Subject matter experts (SMEs) play a prominent role later in their careers as coaches or mentors. They may also develop personal work profiles to help identify the critical at-risk expertise that should be captured and transferred to newer crews. In some cases, the life cycle of the SME extends into retirement, when a former employee may return to work on specific project assignments or serve as a mentor.

8.3 Knowledge Retention and Transfer Processes

The goal of knowledge retention is first to identify the critical skills, experience, and relationships that are at risk when experts retire or transfer, and second to ensure that younger employees who assume subject matter experts' (SMEs') responsibilities acquire the know-how necessary for continuing success. Many companies possess knowledge management strategies. Considering their business goals, they deploy processes or tools such as communities of practice (CoPs), best-practice repositories, or after-action reviews. These processes are easily adaptable for retention and transfer.

Not all processes are equally useful for a particular expert or discipline. We have developed a matrix (Table 8.1) that organizes processes and tools in three dimensions: competency goal (competent or expert), time available (weeks or months to years), and the nature of the expertise (explicit or tacit).

The following offers additional explanation of the knowledge retention toolset.

- *Competency*: The greatest impact to a business comes from accelerating the development of new hires to enable them to perform competently with minimal support. However, companies cannot ignore the need to maintain a smaller group of experts that maintain a competitive edge in a technical discipline. Studies have shown that it can take at least 7 to 10 years of concentrated study and practice to become an expert. It may require decades to reach world-class capability. The quest for expertise needs conscious and continuous nurturing.
- *Time Available*: Has your key expert given a 2-month retirement notice, or can you plan for a deliberate, complete transfer of knowledge?
- *Nature of Expertise*: Knowledge gained through years of experience (tacit) can be hard for an expert to articulate.

8.4   The Role of Knowledge Harvesting

Most of Chevron's knowledge retention processes are results of past knowledge management initiatives. Our biggest shortcoming was in the area of capturing vital expertise in a short timeframe, typically just before retirement. This need is addressed by knowledge harvesting.

Knowledge harvesting is one component of an overall knowledge management program, which in turn is one part of a set of processes related to organizational improvement.

Most experts have great difficulty articulating precisely how they produce complex work results. They have internalized their analytical approach over many years and tend to automatically respond to unique situations in nontransparent ways. To help experts make their expertise more explicit, Chevron evaluated and adopted a mature, proven interview-based process developed by Knowledge Harvesting Inc.

One prominent aspect of knowledge harvesting is a collection of methods for eliciting information about four types of knowledge: declarative knowledge, procedural knowledge, contextual knowledge, and social knowledge. Each type of knowledge is associated with a type of information (Table 8.2).

Table 8.1 Knowledge Retention Processes and Tools

Nature of Expertise	Competent Performers		Experts	
	Weeks	*Months, Years*	*Weeks*	*Months, Years*
Explicit	Documentation, interviews	Best-Practices, Training Courses, Embed in Processes and Tools	Not applicable. Expertise is developed over years of hands-on practice.	
Tacit	Outsource, Retiree Program, Knowledge Harvesting	Peer Reviews, Communities Mentoring/Coaching, Knowledge Harvesting, Expert Systems, Job Shadowing, Rotational Assignments	Outsource, Retiree Program, Knowledge Harvesting	Mentoring/Coaching

Table 8.2 Types of Knowledge and Information

Type of Knowledge	Information Harvested	Value, Use
Contextual knowledge	Signals	"Knowing when, knowing why"
Declarative knowledge	Support information	"Knowing about"
Procedural knowledge	Guidance	"Knowing what and how to"
Social knowledge	Collaborative norms	"Knowing how to work with others"

Following is a brief description of the stages of the knowledge harvesting methodology.

1. Focus helps you identify the knowledge in your organization that is most urgent and important to capture. It is important to understand the breadth of the work as well as the organization's priorities.
2. The Find stage provides guidance on locating experts and existing support information. Documents are studied. Excerpts are gathered.
3. Elicit shows you how to conduct effective harvesting sessions. The goal is to carry out effective interviews with the subject matter experts.
4. Organize instructs you on how to make sense of the information collected through interviews and documents. In this stage, identify patterns and organize the knowledge into logical groups of signals, support information, and guidance.
5. During the Package stage, you determine the best vehicle for packaging the knowledge so that it can be transferred to others. Determine how best to apply the know-how. If working with a retiring worker, often the packaging stage results in a living system which offers guidance, structure, and a living resource for present and future performance support.
6. Evaluate provides tools and guidance for measuring the effectiveness, efficiency, and adaptability of the knowledge assets or living system.
7. Adapt provides tools and guidance for adapting harvesting results to better meet the emerging needs of target learners.

8.5 Case Study: Capturing and Transferring a Complex Technical Process

One Chevron business unit faced an increasingly common challenge: the average age of its technical staff was well over 50 years. Many were nearing retirement, and few new employees were ready to take their place. Dave, a chemist responsible for analyzing fuel product quality, had announced plans to retire in a few months. He played a key role in support of refining, marketing, and supply/trading business

Table 8.3   Contents of a Work Profile

Work Profile Content	Description
Deliverables ("results")	What are your major work results (products, services, and expertise)?
Key stakeholders	Who are your customers and other stakeholders?
Suppliers and personal network	Who helps you get your job done and what do they provide?
Tools and information resources	What resources are required to help you accomplish your work?
Projects	What are your major projects?
List of work process and subprocesses	Map out your work processes and subprocesses. What is your role?
List of safety issues	What safety practices or procedures are relevant to your work?

units. While several other members of the technical staff were familiar with his analytic methods, they lacked his more than 20 years of experience in fine-tuning the method, creating numerous reports that extracted and formatted key information relevant to specific requests, and learning how to recognize and interpret patterns in complex analytical results.

The Knowledge Harvesting project began by developing Dave's work profile. This high-level summary helps Dave and his stakeholders prioritize the unique, critical results that will be at risk when he retires. The contents of a complete work profile are shown in Table 8.3.

The following sections describe key aspects of the knowledge harvesting work that we accomplished with Dave.

8.5.1   Focus

The expert's major deliverables are a good place to initiate the Focus stage of knowledge harvesting. We assembled a fairly complete list of Dave's deliverables using his most recent annual performance plan and several project plans. We then asked Dave's key stakeholders (customers, colleagues, and managers) to select the work results that matter most to their business. We identified three critical knowledge areas:

1. Product quality and performance evaluation.
2. Purchased fuel qualification.
3. Refinery processing effects on hydrocarbon stream.

Table 8.4 Examples of Interview Questions

Orientation	Examples of Questions
General questions	What knowledge do you think is most likely to vanish when you retire? What is unique about your background compared to other employees in positions like yours? What are some key lessons you have learned? Any illustrative stories to tell? For those key projects in your career, which ones were successes and why, in your opinion? Which ones were failures and why?
Technically oriented questions	What are the common problems? How do patterns differ between common and unusual or rare problems? Are there other signals you look for to help interpret the data? How do you know when the results are suspect? Are there any special techniques for streamlining the process? How do you use knowledge of manufacturing processes and product specifications to help troubleshoot quality and performance problems?
Questions about target learners	What suggestions do you have to facilitate the transition to new employees? When you started in this position, what do you wish you had been told?

As the critical knowledge areas were identified, we aligned them with the business' goals, pertinent operating as well as support processes, and performance indicators.

8.5.2 Find

Harvesters must be skilled at asking good questions, because they typically do not have in-depth understanding of the expert's domain. During the Find stage, the expert is asked to provide background information to help the interviewer grasp key concepts. Dave provided examples of recent analytical reports matching the critical knowledge areas. Dave's documentation was used to produce a hypothesized list of his thinking processes as well as ideas for how to embed the knowledge into work processes.

From this information, a starter set of interview questions was developed for the Elicit stage of the process. Table 8.4 gives a few examples of questions.

8.5.3   Elicit

The core strength of the harvesting process lies in helping the expert articulate how good work results are produced. During a week-long engagement, we asked Dave to walk through a number of customer requests. Rather than simply capturing how he worked, we sought Dave's explicit guidance about the details of his thinking and decision making. In particular, we captured information about why certain steps were important and what signals indicated when and how to act.

We quickly recognized one central element for much of his work—his hydrocarbon analytical method. He would ask the customer a set of framing questions designed to illuminate particular characteristics of the fuel sample (for example, grade and source) and available information about the refinery processing used in its manufacture. This information helped him to select the appropriate analytical reports to run. Armed with the necessary knowledge, Dave was then able to look for specific patterns in spreadsheet reports that would create an accurate representation of the complex hydrocarbon mixture present in the sample. Considering the composition of the mixture, Dave was able to explain current quality and performance problems as well as predict future ones.

An understanding of an SME's work may need to include components of which the expert is not even aware. Several days into the interviews, we asked Dave to review a six-step process that we constructed. Initially, he rejected the model. He said that the process we had described did not properly represent his methods. Instead of carefully following all the steps we had identified, he consciously thought through the first few steps, generated the required data and jumped directly to the interpretation. Over his 20 years' experience he had internalized so much of his thinking that he could easily recognize patterns and associate them with problems he had worked on before.

However, when we asked Dave to work through several new examples using our elicited process, he found that it captured his mental model quite accurately. He was able to expand some of the alternatives in the initial process steps to cover problem areas that we had not previously discussed. We then shared the process with a few peers and two technicians, who commented that the captured process helped them better to understand their work.

Sometimes a variety of media can prove useful in eliciting and transferring appropriate knowledge. In our experience (and that of many colleagues), videotapes of interview sessions typically fail to add significant value for new learners; video documentation is more difficult to catalog and search. In Dave's case, however, we found a very useful video approach.

While discussing Dave's process for analyzing data, we watched him navigate through spreadsheets to reveal how the relative values of columns of numbers corresponded to specific types of hydrocarbons in the sample. We found it extremely useful to record Dave reviewing his analysis of the spreadsheets using screen capture software. The resulting set of 5-minute vignettes was immensely effective; even the experienced technicians were able to gain significant insight into the data they produced. Finally, Dave's replacement found these videos invaluable to his competency development.

A mental model which entails complex thinking processes is a common characteristic of deep expertise. It explains why an expert may find it so difficult to share the work process, and why newer employees often struggle to develop competency. Once the thinking process has been converted to an explicit approach, it becomes a practical learning aid. This method is the end goal of knowledge harvesting. A new hire will not become a competent performer overnight. The mental model has distilled the expert's years of experience into a framework that the successor can use to better organize each new work request and, through experience, accelerate the ability to associate patterns, decisions, and interpretations.

8.5.4 Organize, Package

The most labor-intensive part of the process includes transcribing the interviews and reviewing documents provided by the expert. The harvester assembles the content in a context that aligns with the needs of the target learners. One must explore several key categories of knowledge assets. First is documentation about the work results. This includes step-by-step guidance covering the what, how, when, and why. We also identify the expert's personal network, including customers and their typical requests, as well as other internal or external experts that can provide key information outside the expert's discipline.

Examples of deliverables created during this project are listed below. Having this information will aid the effects of turnover, especially when the expert is no longer available.

- Work profile that details key job responsibilities, project summaries, categorized list of customer requests, and a list of upcoming projects with succinct explanations and a quarter-by-quarter schedule for the next few years
- "Living system" of learning and performance-support resources with in-depth analysis and interpretation of hydrocarbon composition data (including video), procedures for handling common requests (e.g., sample collection and characterization), and a systematic analytical approach
- Model depicting the interrelationships among the variables of hydrocarbon analyses
- Explicit links between projects, work results, customers/suppliers/experts, and tools
- Cross-company/functional view of activities and decisions that occur over the life of a fuel sample including important resources, key contacts (personal network), analytical process documentation, and a catalog of useful information resources

8.5.5 Expert's Review and Comments

The contributing expert's verbatim comments were as follows:

- *This would not have worked if I was asked to write this up without the interviewer. He enabled me to just sit and talk. I didn't have to figure it out. His probing questions were essential in helping me come up with relevant examples and explanations. A form or template wouldn't have helped much.*
- *We covered the whole scope of what I do that is uniquely mine as a fuel chemist and how I operate within the framework of my business unit and with our customers. This exceeded my expectations.*
- *It was helpful that in the past we were encouraged to write up and regularly review project statements. This was good background for my work profile. The overall knowledge capture we did covers not only the high-level context of my work but also low-level details of how to do it.*
- *The videos were very powerful. I've been asked to write down my thought process and how I synthesize my responses and guidance as I analyze a hydrocarbon analysis report. The screen capture tool allowed me to do this in a very short time. I couldn't have done it any other way.*
- *One shortcoming is the short timeframe. This knowledge asset will need to be edited, validated, and extended and will improve when allowed to mature with use by my successor.*

8.5.6 Peers' and Stakeholders' Evaluation and Comments

The expert's peers and stakeholders evaluated the knowledge harvesting deliverables and offered these comments:

- *This will be a big help to enable us to create an initial assessment for the customers. The videos are particularly useful. In reviewing the work I concentrated on the value for newcomers. Would the language be understandable? I found that you don't need to be a Ph.D. to understand the documents; they were very clear. (Technician)*
- *It is a little like taking a college course. But in this case, I am applying it directly to my job. (Technician)*
- *The overall package looks like a very powerful approach. It is important to have the replacement available for some overlapping period to ensure continuity of the work (Note: In this case, we did not have that opportunity to include the replacement in the knowledge harvesting interviews). Dave's work is detailed and subtle. It may take a year to get the new person adequately up-to-speed. (Supervisor)*
- *It is valuable to have the new protégé participate in the harvesting process. This significantly accelerates associated mentoring. The protégé picks up the ability to ask good questions. (Knowledge Harvesting Interviewer)*

■ *I was skeptical about the value of this project. That they were able to get to the heart of the systematic analytical approach is fantastic and exceeded my expectations. I'm impressed with what has been developed in the short amount of time. (Manager)*
■ *This won't teach someone to be Dave. There are still many intangible nuances that he has developed over years of experience; these are the hardest, perhaps impossible, things to transfer. In terms of the fundamentals, it looks like we have something very valuable. We need to consider this for future opportunities. (Manager)*
■ *Utterly invaluable. (Dave's successor, hired several months after Dave retired)*

8.6 Chevron's Experience with Knowledge Harvesting

Chevron's experience with knowledge harvesting began in 2006. The following sections offer information about our lessons learned as well as the value achieved.

8.6.1 Lessons Learned

Table 8.5 lists Chevron's observations about knowledge harvesting.

8.6.2 Knowledge Harvesting—A Useful Addition to Chevron's Knowledge Retention Toolkit

Business-critical knowledge ranges from well-documented practices to hard-to-articulate experience. New employees also have differing preferences in their styles of learning. There is no one-size-fits-all knowledge retention solution; a variety of methods will be necessary to educate the next generation of Chevron employees. A good set of processes and the appropriate guidance for when to use them is an important management resource.

Two reasons explain why knowledge harvesting is becoming an important part of our toolkit. One reason is time: the number of SME retirements will escalate over the next few years, and our existing transfer tools are not well-adapted to short turnover cycles. A more important reason is the end result: the distillation of years of expertise into a learning framework that helps new practitioners think through their work and more quickly identify patterns and associated interpretations and decisions.

This knowledge transfer process does not scale very well. Knowledge harvesting[*] is an intricate process and is not appropriate for every employee. Managers typically know which individuals have critical expertise. Knowledge harvesting engagements should focus on these experts who contribute to operational effectiveness.

---

[*] *Note*: "Knowledge Harvesting" is a registered trademark of Knowledge Harvesting Inc.

Table 8.5   Chevron's Observations about Knowledge Harvesting

Observation	Description
Expert's attitude	The expert needs to be interested in sharing expertise and have patience when dealing with the interviewer's questions. We have found that most experts are genuinely engaged by the process.
Expert's preparation	Experts who have good job documentation practices can significantly facilitate the work.
At-risk expertise	We have captured experts' systems thinking (mental models) as well as detailed guidance based on signals that trigger experts' decision making. This information goes beyond what is typically captured in knowledge documentation, and its complexity requires a skilled interviewer. In particular, knowledge harvesting works effectively with complex knowledge and should be considered for SMEs who possess critical at-risk expertise.
Focus	Having a neutral third party familiar with the business and the technical domain will help make sure the elicitation is focused on the most vital topics.
Interviewer's persistence	Continued probing to get more details and examples on how and why certain complex thinking tasks were accomplished resulted in valuable information.
Interviewer's assimilation time	Understanding the constructs and jargon of a new discipline takes time. This may not fully occur until after interviews are completed. In some situations, spreading interviews over several weeks or months may help with awareness and allow subsequent interview sessions to probe deeper into the subject matter.
Capture tools	On-screen videos with voice-over is another effective capture tool to use when an expert should provide explanations of how certain information tools fit into everyday workflow.

There are however two harvesting tools that can be implemented broadly without requiring extensive knowledge transfer skills:

■ Asking good questions is a teachable but overlooked capability. It can improve knowledge transfer in mentoring engagements.
■ Work profiling can be broadly applied throughout the organization. Work profiles provide an excellent focal point for discussions which occur during planned job turnover.

A full suite of knowledge retention processes coupled with the leadership vision to know where and when to use them will help Chevron minimize business disruption and maximize competency development in the years ahead. Making expert thinking visible benefits all employees, not just the "next crew." Competency and solid, risk-based decision making are critical to performing safely and with excellence.

Chapter 9

The Aerospace Corporation Case Study

Stewart Sutton, Joseph Betser,
Mary Hornickel, Michelle Gregorio,
Jeffery Kern, Christine Lincoln, and Jovel Crisostomo
The Aerospace Corporation Knowledge Management Office

9.1 Introduction

Since its founding almost 50 years ago, The Aerospace Corporation (Aerospace) has been a premier knowledge-based company [1]. As the operator of a federally funded research and development center (FFRDC), or the "system engineer" for National Security Space (NSS), Aerospace offers knowledge as its principal product to the customers it serves. Unique challenges exist for organizations that are formed to assure the stewardship of knowledge, and this chapter provides an account of how Aerospace has managed its stewardship obligations as the operator of the nation's FFRDC for national security space programs.

9.2 Company Background

The Aerospace Corporation was established in 1960 as a California nonprofit corporation dedicated to space mission success and government service. For almost 50 years, Aerospace has operated as an FFRDC sponsored by the Office of the Under Secretary of the Air Force. The Aerospace FFRDC contract is managed by the U.S.

Air Force Space and Missile Systems Center at the Los Angeles Air Force Base, California. Aerospace is governed by a board of trustees and in 2007 had a total staff of more than 3800 employees (including a technical staff of 2600) in facilities throughout the nation and earned more than $800 million in revenue.

There are five principal functions, or core competencies, of the corporation's FFRDC: (1) launch certification, (2) system-of-systems engineering, (3) systems development and acquisition, (4) process implementation, and (5) technology application. Each of these principal functions is delivered through the coordinated actions of the Aerospace staff working in close collaboration with its customers:

1. Launch certification has no room for error, because failures are very costly in financial terms and in schedule impact. Aerospace staff provides validation services as part of flight vehicle processing. A series of highly complex reviews combined with technical and programmatic analysis are coordinated to certify readiness for flight.
2. System-of-systems engineering addresses the significant challenges inherent in the detailed architecture and planning of space systems and their relationship to other equally complex system assets located in the air, on the ground, and at sea. This class of engineering and design requires Aerospace to affect deep simulation, analysis, and careful assessments at each stage to assure mission success.
3. Systems development and acquisition are accomplished by working with Aerospace's government sponsors to assure requirements for space systems are properly clarified in advance of design and procurement. An essential part of that clarification is the risk and performance assessment associated with the overall system design and its respective components.
4. Process implementation assures that military specifications, standards, and associated process developments are consistent, complete, and appropriate to the domain of national security space.
5. Technology application addresses the need to assess technology opportunities, alternatives, and risks associated with space systems and their supporting infrastructure.

9.2.1 A History of Knowledge Retention (1960 to Present)

For true effectiveness, stewardship of knowledge should align with the principal functions of an organization. With that in mind, Aerospace established early on the knowledge stewardship function within the framework of corporate technical reports that are authored by members of the technical staff (MTS). These technical reports provide key insights and guidance to Aerospace customers, serving as a written record of the many technical oversight functions for which Aerospace MTS are responsible in relationship to a broad array of space systems. Sometimes these oversight functions require a top-level review of systems in design, development, or test. At other times, MTS must validate their opinions and knowledge through the construction of artifacts. These artifacts can be components of space system hardware, space and ground systems software, or they may represent highly complex simulations with accompanying analysis. In all cases, the result of such artifacts (their construction and assessment) is to provide unbiased information to MTS so that they may record their insights and guidance in the corporate reports that are ultimately delivered to Aerospace customers.

9.2.2   The Knowledge Management Role of the Aerospace Library and Information Resources Center

The Charles C. Lauritsen Library was established at the birth of Aerospace to collect and provide access to the scientific and technical literature necessary to support the corporate mission. In addition to archival retention of codified corporate knowledge, the library has always provided professional knowledge services. These services include knowledge location services (whether the knowledge is internal or external to the company), knowledge organization services (in the form of the library catalog and company thesaurus), and knowledge dissemination. Library staff, with advanced information management degrees, works closely with subject matter experts to assist them with their secondary research. Over time, the library staff has become the "best Rolodex in the company"—an informal expertise locator service by virtue of "knowing who knows what."

Materials in the corporate archives include papers, maps, photographs, and other documents created by the company dating back to the 1960s. The Aerospace-generated technical report collection consists of over 105,000 reports dating back to the company's formation. So vital is this wealth of materials that the Air Force informally refers to Aerospace as its corporate memory and has formally designated the library's pre-1970 collection of external reports as an Air Force historical collection.

Today, Aerospace considers its Library and Information Resources Center to be a national treasure. Several members of the Library and Information Resource Center staff are embedded in program offices where they assist in managing knowledge specific to that organization. New knowledge responsibilities assigned to the library staff include leading training activities for the organization's cadre of corporate knowledge stewards, leading the Knowledge Steward Community of Practice, and providing stewardship in initiating and guiding the formation and conduct of Aerospace's various communities. The library recently launched a storytelling series, in which retired executives share their involvement in and insights about the history and key decisions of the National Security Space program.

In addition, the Library and Information Resources Center was a founding member of the corporate Knowledge Management Steering Team in 1999, commissioned by the company's executive vice president to provide recommendations for comprehensive knowledge management at Aerospace.

9.2.3 Knowledge Management within Aerospace-at-Large

9.2.3.1   1960s and 1970s

In the 1960s and 1970s the exchange of knowledge between staff occurred principally through face-to-face meetings and through shared written (paper-based) material. Multiparticipant meetings were typical in the 1960s and are still common today. Group collaboration has been an essential part of material refinement since the company's beginning. Since its founding, Aerospace has employed some of the leading experts in many fields of study that support the principal functions of the company. These recognized experts are typically the key authors of the corporate reports, but the full authorship is often much broader. In the early days, multiple contributors hand-wrote material to be typed and proofread by company secretaries. These typed reports were subject to peer review as part of the corporate reports process. Upon successful peer review (incorporating required changes and feedback from various stakeholders), the reports would be signed off by corporate management as an endorsement of the material's accuracy and completeness.

Conversion to electronic document formats has generally improved the stewardship of materials at Aerospace. Initially, it was simply typewriter and filing cabinet. Throughout the 1960s, the technical staff was accountable for retaining the materials they authored, which were filed into personal or departmental filing cabinets. The secretarial staff greatly facilitated this filing operation. In the 1980s the stewardship role shifted slightly; in fact, it was a foreshadowing of what would emerge in 2005. The fledgling word processing infrastructure allowed the secretarial staff to take part in an early form of electronic stewardship of reports. They were the true stewards of the electronic reports in the word processing system, but because the electronic system was not a *recognized* system of record, the secretaries' stewardship skills were largely directed at the efficiency of creating reports that integrated author content from multiple technical areas within the company. This practice would also foreshadow similar electronic collaboration by authors nearly 20 years later.

9.2.3.2   1980s

The introduction of word processing "systems" in the early 1980s changed the role of the secretary in the corporation. Recall that the first word processing systems were centralized systems that existed prior to the company-wide deployment of personal computers. Since its founding in 1960, Aerospace has always owned sophisticated computers for scientists and engineers to use for complex modeling and simulation, but with the 1980s came a new computing capability in the form of a centralized word processing system. This new product allowed the secretarial staff to record the corporate reports into a system as part of their typing effort, vastly improving efficiency. This also improved productivity, since revising material stored on an electronic system took a fraction of the time needed to make manual corrections. What was even more profound was the role that the secretary would have in relationship to material stewardship. While not the expert in the material domain, the secretarial network had the keys to the material stored within the company-wide shared word processing system. Soon the corporate secretaries were collaborating with one another on the exchange of electronic materials, further improving the peer review actions required by MTS. In short, this was a wonderful system. The focus on material content was the duty of staff experts, while the focus on material recording and presentation was the responsibility of the corporate secretary and, for the really important material, a dedicated staff within the corporate communications department. Aerospace had a highly functional system for knowledge management, and yet it would not fully appreciate the distinct roles of authorship and stewardship until many years later.

By the mid-1980s, something new called the "personal computer" (PC) was introduced at Aerospace; it would have a profound impact on the stewardship model in place. With a PC, each MTS could now take complete control of his or her own material. This technology infusion continued to accelerate the efficiency of corporate reporting; however, all MTS would discover that, in addition to typing their own material, they would now be responsible for ongoing *electronic* stewardship of that material. Previously, stewardship of material had been structured around physical file cabinets filled with paper reports, and the task had typically been left to the secretarial staff. The introduction of electronic stewardship did not immediately replace the paper-based stewardship in place. In fact, parallel stewardship of both paper and electronic items continues today. There is considerably more material on the electronic side of the spectrum, and most critical legacy material has been converted to electronic form. Additionally, all new materials are developed and retained in electronic formats.

9.2.3.3 1990s to 2007

From the 1990s into the 2000s, the knowledge stewardship process had adapted substantially to support electronic infrastructure. There are still many occasions where formulating the right opinion and delivering the best knowledge requires construction of space flight hardware and software systems to help validate concepts. However, some concept validations that once required physical artifacts can now be done via simulation. High-fidelity modeling and simulation tools have dramatically expanded in capability in proportion to the complexity of systems for which Aerospace has oversight. As a result, corporate reports now integrate even more complex material, with multiple perspectives and deeper analysis than in prior years. Report writing still follows the sequence where the principal and secondary author(s) craft a report, peers and stakeholders review it, and management ultimately endorses and approves the report for publication. What has emerged over the last 5 years is a variety of new forms of collaboration afforded by the electronic infrastructure. The most advanced forms of electronic collaboration provided by wiki technology and Google documents are introducing a new type of multiparticipant parallel authoring that is radically different from the traditional cycle described earlier. Time will tell if massively parallel authoring takes hold within other organizations that are producers of knowledge.

Knowledge stewardship and retention are driven to deliver the right information within the proper context to address a specific issue at the appropriate time. The modern institutional repository of corporate reports and other stored electronic materials provides a baseline for material stewardship. In years past, materials were stored in paper form, and the stewardship of knowledge-on-paper was considered inefficient. For one thing, a physical search for such material was only as good as the individuals who remembered what was there and knew where to find it. On the positive side, material was at least well organized. As organizations have moved into the digital information age, a key part of stewardship demands that we consistently mark and label the material that enters the digital library, to facilitate easy retrieval. These marks and labels aid in the search and discovery of what is there, and they also serve as key indicators of what is recognized as pedigree knowledge within the organization. Without an organizational process and supporting structure that help to differentiate key material from other digital documents within the system of record, the path to authoritative source material is unclear. We may then find that a large digital library presents more of a burden than a benefit.

There is also an ongoing shift in perspective related to who the participants are in the stewardship of organizational knowledge. At the most basic level, knowledge is a personal thing. Our training and experience allow us to understand; from that understanding, we are able to chart a course of action. How well we follow that course, and the resulting outcomes, are indicators of how knowledgeable we are within the field we support. Still, we know that our contributions must be integrated into the broader knowledge of the organization. In this way, we become more than individual contributors within a group of intelligent knowledge workers. By integrating our contributions, the process takes us from a focus on personal stewardship, beyond group-level departmental stewardship and into corporate stewardship. A corporate-level stewardship perspective is a prerequisite to achieving effective cross-discipline knowledge retention (see Figure 9.1).

Aerospace increasingly seeks to share its knowledge with others (as appropriate) via the exchange of digital information. Ironically, some of the greatest benefits of digital information sharing also present some of the most difficult challenges. For one thing, digital information exchange occurs quickly—and while the benefit of "quick" can greatly facilitate internal peer review, it can also facilitate the

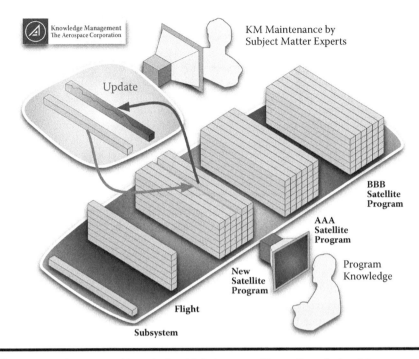

Figure 9.1 Aerospace Knowledge Maintenance (From *Knowledge Management at The Aerospace Corporation—A 50 Year Journey*, p. 13. Copyright 2008 by The Aerospace Corporation. With permission.)

unintentional release of draft materials to an audience that may overlook or not realize the material has not been finalized. And once the information has been released, there's no getting it back. To use an e-mail analogy, there is no "return what I sent out" button in one's e-mail system. Structured, permission-based wikis and other enterprise content management systems with predefined permissions frameworks can help with many of the electronic stewardship/access issues by prompting both knowledge providers and would-be recipients to ensure the information is appropriate for dissemination and the readers are authorized to receive it. Bottom line, the guidelines that safeguard the step-by-step methods for knowledge sharing are just as important as the technology that they reference.

9.3 Knowledge Management Initiatives at Aerospace

Numerous knowledge management activities are coordinated within a knowledge management strategic initiative at Aerospace. This initiative was made a permanent fixture of company operations in 2006 through an administrative budget allocation specifically directed at the continued improvement and institutionalization of

Figure 9.2   Knowledge Management Governance (From *Knowledge Management at The Aerospace Corporation—A 50 Year Journey,* p. 15. Copyright 2008 by The Aerospace Corporation. With permission.)

knowledge management technology and processes. This and other knowledge management initiatives at Aerospace are integrated within a knowledge management roadmap that is managed by the company's Knowledge Management Office. The overarching governance for knowledge management is provided by both a reporting relationship to the company's information office and a key stakeholder relationship that knowledge management holds with the company's "customer council." This council is composed of the major internal business segment representatives throughout Aerospace (see Figure 9.2).

The Aerospace Knowledge Management Roadmap (see Figure 9.3) is divided into a handful of topic areas. For each topic area, there is an intended outcome and objective. Individual topics are activity and project aggregators, and the collective activity and initiatives within the topic area represent the total scope of the knowledge management initiatives within the company.

Some of the current key knowledge management initiatives at Aerospace include:

- Communities for collaboration and stewardship
- Enterprise-wide knowledge search
- Expertise location within the enterprise
- Mission assurance tools and frameworks

9.3.1   Communities for Stewardship

In 2005, Aerospace initiated a broad "communities initiative," whose principal objective was to address cross-organizational stewardship of material when the contributing experts to that material were not isolated within a single organizational department or section. Addressing cross-organizational, long-term stewardship of

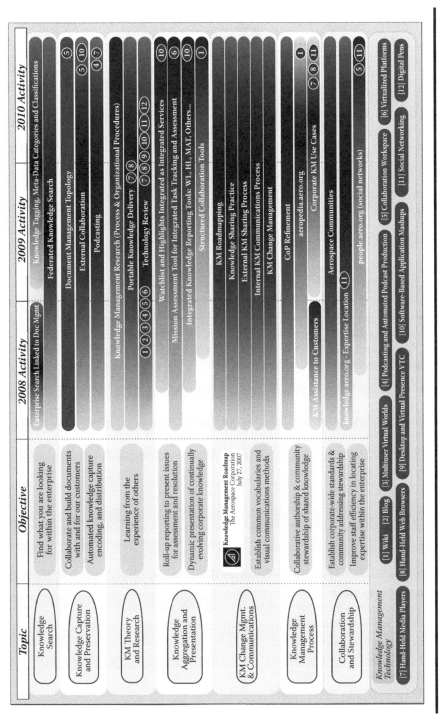

Figure 9.3 Knowledge Management Roadmap (From *Knowledge Management at The Aerospace Corporation—A 50 Year Journey*, p. 16. Copyright 2008 by The Aerospace Corporation. With permission.)

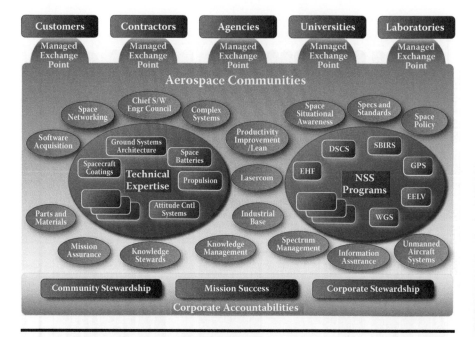

Figure 9.4 Aerospace Communities of Practice (From *Knowledge Management at The Aerospace Corporation—A 50 Year Journey*, p. 17. Copyright 2008 by The Aerospace Corporation. With permission.)

technical content in this manner was coordinated through two complementary frameworks: communities of practice (CoPs) and communities of interest (CoIs) (see Figure 9.4).

A CoI is a grassroots formulation of staff who come together on a common interest and share knowledge for the collective benefit of the membership. Within a CoI, there is no mandated formality around knowledge stewardship. The CoI members have suggested guidelines on sharing knowledge, but there is limited review of that sharing activity. The institutional repository for document sharing is made available to CoIs, and if there is zero activity within a fiscal year, all of the material within that area is archived. The CoI members can retrieve material from the archive with a simple request. New CoIs are compared against existing CoIs to prevent duplication of effort. This comprises the total level of oversight within the CoI type of community.

A CoP provides a more formal stewardship framework for the corporation. Each CoP has a mandated governance framework of defined roles within the community. Each CoP provides a formal charter, list of roles and responsibilities, topics, and a near-term roadmap. The CoP is recognized by Aerospace as having an influential voice, and its members may collaborate to form and author "community positions" on its topics. This community position has increased value because of

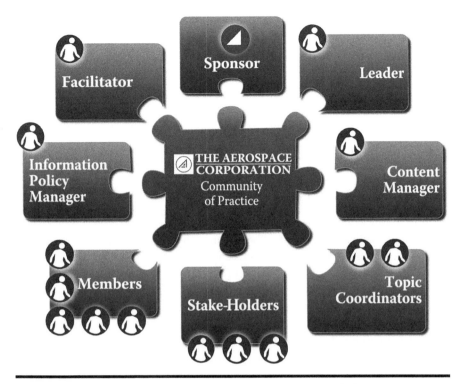

Figure 9.5 Community of Practice Leadership (From *Knowledge Management at The Aerospace Corporation—A 50 Year Journey*, p. 18. Copyright 2008 by The Aerospace Corporation. With permission.)

the defined process for position formulation, peer review, and approval set forth within the CoP. A CoP position on a particular topic can be more easily published as a corporate position because of the rigor the CoP follows in position formulation. The formal roles within a CoP play a vital role in the quality of knowledge sharing. Following is a list of defined roles within a CoP (also see Figure 9.5):

1. *Sponsor*—Each CoP has a senior executive sponsor who is responsible for the strategic value of the CoP.
2. *Leader*—The CoP leader sets the direction and emphasis for the community. The leader is also accountable for the performance of the community.
3. *Facilitator*—The facilitator helps to ensure that the community dialogue and participation engage the full diversity of the member and stakeholder participants.
4. *Content Manager*—The content manager oversees the full collection of community material that is shared within a common community repository.
5. *Information policy manager*—The information policy manager ensures that access to and release of material outside the community meets appropriate legal, contractual, corporate, and government guidelines.

6. *Topic Coordinator(s)*—Topic coordinators are responsible for leading the material development on specific topics overseen by the community.
7. *Stakeholders*—Stakeholders are all parties that have an interest in the material and opinions developed by the community.
8. *Members*—Members of a CoP must maintain active participation in the formulation of community material or community positions.

9.3.2   Knowledge Search

Aerospace has always recognized the importance of organizing and reusing knowledge. The recognition of the company's collective knowledge as the real value of Aerospace can be seen in three levels of knowledge preservation:

1. Aerospace has had a robust library function since its inception. Encompassing the archives, records retention center, and the research library, the Library and Information Resources Center is the corporate entity mandated to record and archive all formal reports deliverable pursuant to active contracts. Developed in large part on an academic model, the library provides a balance of both printed and electronic resources in support of the company's principal functions. In addition to a fully integrated online library system, the library manages a wide array of full-text electronic resources available to all employees' desktops, as well as a full-service repository housing all relevant print resources. While every effort is made to provide access to knowledge in user-friendly formats, the library also provides personalized research services from a staff of aerospace industry-focused information professionals to ensure expert location of both internal and external knowledge.
2. Aerospace's document management software, AeroLink, serves as a secondary knowledge preservation and sharing tool. AeroLink contains organizational knowledge folders, community workspaces, and collections of formal corporate reports, specifications, standards, other technical documents, and collaboration spaces. Digitization of large collections of formerly print-only collections has made deep resources of both current and historical knowledge readily retrievable for use.
3. Knowledge also resides at the departmental level in wikis, portals, and local collections unique to the various highly specialized technical disciplines required to fulfill the company's mission. These knowledge tools are often more closely held and shared within laboratory mentoring environments.

9.3.3   Expertise Location

As the primary knowledge support for the Space and Missile Systems Center, Aerospace provides expertise in a number of aerospace and related engineering skills. The corporate organizational structure was created at inception to facilitate this. Organizationally, Aerospace has several program offices that work hand in hand with the Air Force and other customers. Supporting the program offices is the Engineering Technology Group (ETG), which is organized by engineering expertise. Members matrix to multiple program offices, thereby supporting multiple national space programs and transferring knowledge between them. For example, if a particular bus fails on a NASA spacecraft supported by Aerospace, the company broadcasts that knowledge to Air Force spacecraft programs that use the same or similar buses.

Program office personnel locate ETG experts in multiple ways. One significant way is using the *ETG Functional Guide*, a document that delineates which organizations provide which expertise. The ETG head office provides a general support number for personnel and customers to request expertise. Experts can also be identified by searching Aerospace's extensive published documentation maintained by the Library and Information Resource Center. Finally, as with all mature organizations, there persists the traditional three-phone-call approach to expertise location, wherein managers typically call other managers to find experts. In these situations, an expert can usually be identified and qualified within three phone calls.

Over the past two decades, there have been several attempts to establish additional automated tools to support expertise location at Aerospace. All of these have been unsuccessful ultimately, due to burdensome user requirements to maintain data, privacy issues, or the lack of appropriately simple yet powerful technology. In recent years, technology has progressed sufficiently that new efforts are now underway to provide automated tools to assist internal expertise location.

9.3.4 Mission Assurance Tools and Frameworks

Aerospace has contributed to the successful performance of critical missions by national security space systems for nearly 50 years. Effective mission assurance is critical because space is an unforgiving business—mission failures in the 1990s alone resulted in $11 billion in lost assets. Many of these losses were attributed to the use of nonvalidated acquisition practices—the "faster, better, cheaper" approach that became popular after the end of the Cold War. More significant than the loss in dollars was the loss of vital military and intelligence capabilities and opportunities for space exploration, research, and commerce. Since 1999, the national security space industry has been recovering from those losses by reestablishing tried-and-true practices that emphasize mission success over schedule and cost reduction. This "back-to-basics" approach recognizes that optimum cost performance results from doing the job right the first time and achieving 100% mission success.

Aerospace plays a vital role in and shares accountability for the mission assurance of national security space systems. An obvious part of this accountability entails objective assessment and independent monitoring of program executability and, as part of space system acquisition, providing educated, informed buyer guidance to the government. To help the government manage complex space projects, Aerospace has developed tools such as the Aerospace Watch List and Launch Verification Matrix. Other automation systems in development include the Integrated Mission Assessment Tool. Each of these systems helps to guide the collective expertise of the Aerospace scientists and engineers as they do their work. Furthermore, these mission assurance tools are doing something that has never been done within the company—they are providing a guiding framework for recording evidence during the long and complex process of space system oversight. Using these tools, Aerospace MTS coordinate, monitor, and directly participate in independent program assessments, working alongside contractors in their own facilities.

Each satellite program is now developing, refining, and tailoring its own mission assessment framework. The mission assessment framework seeks to deliver mission success through documented process and the capture of technical evidences for launch and operation readiness. Each portion of the mission assurance framework is assigned to separate teams that monitor systems engineering, the mission control system, launch vehicle integration, systems effectiveness, the space segment (payload and spacecraft bus), information assurance, international partners, and operations. The teams meet regularly to discuss progress of the respective mission assurance tasks and milestones, documentation, and evidence that support decisions, rationale, task completions, and any deviations or exceptions. The Integrated Mission Assessment Tool tracks progress, and supporting documentation is captured in an electronic archive. In aggregate, the assessments provide a clear record that supports the statement, "All requirements have been met, and this satellite is ready to launch."

Aerospace also has developed a comprehensive Mission Assurance Plan that integrates the parallel activities of task reporting and comprehensive assessment. The space systems assurance processes developed over the past 40 years are being refined and automated within a custom-developed enterprise application. The Mission Assurance Plan diagram (see Figure 9.6) illustrates the relationship between work breakdown structures, tailored task plans for individual space programs, and the coordinated information flow to and from the enterprise data store.

9.4 A Closer Look at Knowledge Retention Efforts

9.4.1 Knowledge Retention in Communities

Knowledge formed within communities is retained and managed by that community. Communities, particularly CoPs, develop various types of knowledge that are shared with the company at large. This knowledge is kept within the community "Wisdom" area and comprises best practices, lessons learned, design guidance, community positions, and corporate specifications and standards.

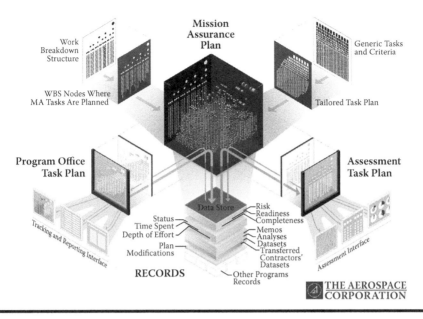

Figure 9.6 Mission Assurance Plan (From *Knowledge Management at The Aerospace Corporation—A 50 Year Journey,* p. 22. Copyright 2008 by The Aerospace Corporation. With permission.)

9.4.2 Knowledge Retention in CoPs

Knowledge within CoPs is developed in a variety of ways, based on the operational model of the community. Strong guidance has been provided by the company's senior leadership around the scope of opinion that must be solicited as part of the knowledge creation process, as well as strict documentation requirements for the CoP's knowledge. No CoP can be considered to have created knowledge worthy of publication as Wisdom unless input has been solicited from a broad spectrum of community members. In addition, thorough documentation of both the majority and the minority opinions developed during this discourse must be retained. The majority opinions are published as Wisdom and, subject to legal limitations, must be available to the corporation as a whole. Minority or "dissenting" views are generally retained and not aired outside the membership of the community, or possibly even the community leadership team. The process for setting CoP positions is shown in Figure 9.7.

9.4.3 Community Wisdom Process (Communities of Practice [CoPs])

Community Wisdom develops either in response to a direct question from a customer or internal management, or proactively, as the community sees a need to

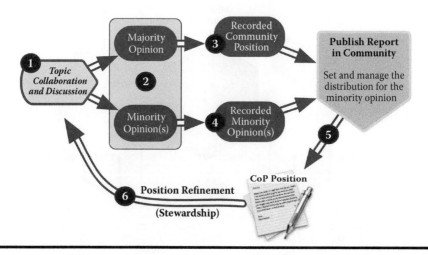

Figure 9.7 Setting CoP Positions (From *Knowledge Management at The Aerospace Corporation—A 50 Year Journey*, p. 23. Copyright 2008 by The Aerospace Corporation. With permission.)

establish guidance in or a position on a particular topical area. Each community develops its own process within the overarching guidelines of appropriate peer review within the community. Elements of this process include the solicitation of input from the community as a whole, review by the community and community leaders, as well as review by community stakeholders. Once a majority position has been reached and approved by the community and its stakeholders, the knowledge becomes community Wisdom. The knowledge publishing process is shown in Figure 9.8. Corporate knowledge is codified in one of the five formal Aerospace report types. The community retains control over the editable-format document, which is filed, with appropriate metadata, into the community Wisdom area. The noneditable format of the document is submitted to the library for permanent retention and archiving. Links are built between the two formats of the document within the corporate document management system. Communities are expected to refresh or at least review their Wisdom documents on a regular basis for ongoing validity or current technical relevance.

9.4.4 Knowledge Retention in Communities of Interest

CoIs have no constraints on the documentation of their knowledge or the processes by which they reach that knowledge, and as such, their positions are not generally seen as "speaking for the company." CoIs are also not required to provide wide access to their Wisdom.

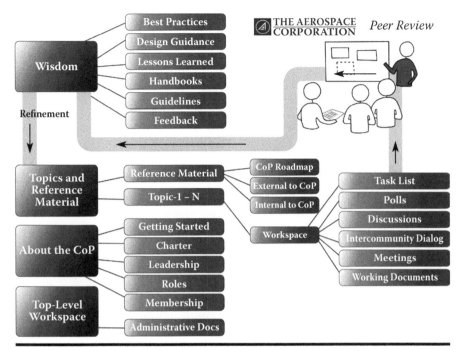

Figure 9.8 Knowledge Publishing in CoPs. (From *Knowledge Management at The Aerospace Corporation—A 50 Year Journey*, p. 24. Copyright 2008 by The Aerospace Corporation. With permission.)

9.4.5 Community Metrics

Community health metrics have been developed to measure a community's progress in building its infrastructure and to measure community activity. Key elements of developing a community infrastructure consist of selecting a leadership team, developing the community membership, outlining topic areas, writing a CoP charter, and building a roadmap. Community activity metrics encompass content growth as evidenced by the number of documents authored and used both by community members and others, usage of Wisdom documents, community participation in meetings and discussions, and community membership growth. Community performance metrics are currently being designed in conjunction with the CoP leaders team. These metrics will focus on the value of the community to Aerospace and its customers.

9.4.6 Technologies for Efficient Knowledge Collaboration, Capture, and Sharing

Technology is constantly being applied to help with the collaboration and stewardship of knowledge. When properly integrated with effective process and procedure, technology can provide effective leverage toward improved collaboration, capture, and sharing of knowledge. There are some very specific technologies under test that are showing promise as Aerospace seeks to improve the efficiency of knowledge collaboration and stewardship. The technologies highlighted here include a document management system, several variations of "wiki" usage, "blogs," and early work in podcast-based command media.

9.4.6.1 Institutional Repository (Document Management)

Document management had been in the "need to fix" category throughout the 1990s. To address the need, in 2002 Aerospace acquired an enterprise-wide document management system as part of the corporate strategic initiative in knowledge management. In the first several years of deployment and tuning, the system met with a fair amount of resistance. This resistance can be attributed to many factors ranging from "complexity of interface" to "change in process." By the third year of the deployment and tuning of the system, pockets of the enterprise were starting to make very effective use of the document management system. The location of documents (as durable URLs) was starting to prove its worth. And while the system for document management has not made radical improvements to collaboration, it achieved solid footing as an enterprise system for ongoing knowledge stewardship of electronic reports. Going forward, document management within a common institutional repository will be considered a core knowledge management capability and an essential foundation to stewardship of electronic documents.

9.4.6.2 Wikis

A wiki is a collaborative Web site that provides an easy way for people to upload and edit information online. Wikis organize data using the concept of "pages" where ideas or topics can be articulated in full, then specific words or segments are linked to related pages for in-depth discussion of a concept. As such, wikis provide a modular way of viewing and storing information while supporting the fact that any piece of information pulls from or relies on other pieces of information.

There are various reasons for using wikis in an organization in terms of knowledge retention, collaboration, and sharing. In particular, the benefits of using a wiki are as follows:

■ Wikis are a Web-based application that is accessible anywhere there is an Internet connection. Information is available on demand. The convenience and usefulness of having information available online in one place so that people can easily search reference articles will hopefully motivate people to move to online authoring. Having information available in a wiki can further assist knowledge stewardship by ensuring that information can be found and eventually archived.

■ Wikis are lightweight software, so multiple instances can be established easily for various purposes. As discussed below, Aerospace plans to deploy wikis for three different types of usage.

■ Wikis allow users to easily create a page and take notes. This feature of wikis is beneficial especially in support of knowledge retention, but it does face a few challenges. Navigating through a wiki is quick and easy if a user has passed the initial learning curve of understanding the use of the wiki and its syntax. The next challenge is convincing people to use the wiki on a regular basis to capture thoughts and ideas so that they will persist. Participation depends greatly on which generation the user is from—typically, the further a person is from the Millennial generation, the less likely they will find the wiki as a useful tool.

■ Wikis track page revisions. This is probably the most useful feature of wikis. Having this functionality allows for a richer collaborative experience, as users can revert to a previous version to fix accidental edits or to revisit an earlier idea. But more importantly, this feature provides a sufficient record of changes and additions to a document, allowing future readers to determine the thought process that went into constructing the article.

■ Wikis give content visibility. Beyond being able to search the content of the wiki, users have a greater chance of finding that something they may not know exists is related to something they are looking for, or could help them with what they are working on by following the linked texts in the page they are reading.

■ Wikis can serve as a place to communicate to the members of the organization. Users and departments can use the wiki as a home for information about themselves so that others can find out more about who they are and what they do. Wikis can also store company processes and how-tos, which is especially useful to new hires seeking to learn more about the organization and how to get things done [2].

Aerospace has deployed or plans to deploy three types of wikis, which will vary in terms of the target audience and how the governance of that wiki is structured. For over 3 years now, Aerospace has hosted a Bulletin Board wiki, which serves as an intranet home page for employees, departments, subdivisions, and divisions. The Bulletin Board wiki is open to everyone in the company to read and author pages. It is an ideal place to host how-tos and synopses about the various projects and activities on which individuals or departments are working.

The second type of wiki that Aerospace plans to deploy is the Team wiki. These are project wikis that are dedicated to a particular project or community team members. Read and write access to this wiki can be restricted to a particular group of people. And though some may be accessible to everyone at Aerospace, it is

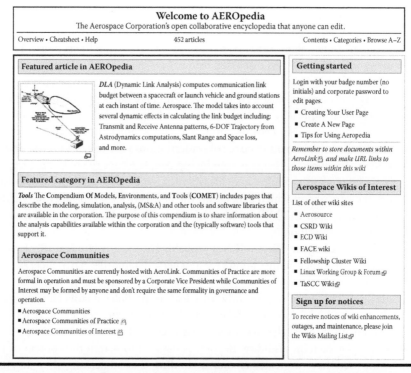

Figure 9.9 Aeropedia Wiki (From *Knowledge Management at The Aerospace Corporation—A 50 Year Journey*, p. 28. Copyright 2008 by The Aerospace Corporation. With permission.)

understood that a Team wiki is meant to be used as a workspace for a specific group to collaborate, coordinate, and draft documents. Currently, the Team wiki is in a cycle of development and experimental deployment. Various groups are using different types of wiki systems to test how well this kind of wiki supports their needs. Aerospace is planning to standardize the Team wiki and create a process where groups can request a wiki to be created for them.

The third type of wiki that is currently under development is Aeropedia (see Figure 9.9). The Aeropedia wiki is meant to serve as a key knowledge source for the company. Aeropedia is open for everyone at Aerospace to read and edit, with a special class of editor associated with "community positions" being restricted to CoP members. The goal is to ensure the quality of content of Aeropedia by governance over the peer-review and authoring protocol. To further ensure quality, Aerospace has refined a governance model with various roles similar to Wikipedia's governance model but with more control on who can author. In Wikipedia, the governance model is meant mainly to handle disputes over content, since everyone can edit. First, users can request assistance from the Mediation Committee to handle dispute over page content [5]. If the Mediation Committee cannot solve

Table 9.1 Aeropedia Governance Roles and Guidelines

Role	Governance Function
Policy manager	Provides guidelines for setting top-level policy. These guidelines are reviewed, modified as needed, and broadly applied by the Aeropedia authors.
Community sponsor	Management oversight for the community wisdom that is published within the Aeropedia wiki.
Community leader	Accountable for a process that allows community members to publish Wisdom into Aeropedia through a defined peer review procedure.
Topic coordinator	Defines page-level community topics that community members may use as organizing pages for their published Wisdom within Aeropedia.
Topic author	A community member who has permissions to place peer reviewed material within Aeropedia.

Source: Knowledge Management at The Aerospace Corporation—A 50 Year Journey, p. 29. Copyright 2008 by The Aerospace Corporation. With permission.

a particular dispute, it is then sent to the Arbitration Committee, which has the authority to make a final decision on any issue [4]. While the committees handle disputes, the quality of content relies heavily on well-meaning editors detecting and fixing erroneous edits or vandalism [3]. Though CoP members at Aerospace can be expected to act as well-meaning editors, content will garner more legitimacy and authority if it is known to have gone through peer review and if the topics written have been determined as useful to Aerospace in fulfilling its function to provide guidance to its customers.

The Aeropedia roles mimic those found in CoPs. The only difference is the policy manager role, which is fulfilled by those who are in charge of authoring guidelines for Aeropedia. A summary of the different Aeropedia roles and functions is shown in Table 9.1.

Content in Aeropedia is meant to function as position papers that members of Aerospace can reference to make decisions. Currently, position papers are signed off by management after going through peer review, and after that point, an assumption holds that the paper will not change anymore. This, in a way, is contrary to the wiki content model where the latest version is the "official" version, with an assumption that this can change at any time. It may be that certain position papers should be allowed to change after it has been approved by management, but with an understanding that the latest revision is not the official position of the company. To solve this, Aerospace may eventually need to custom-build a wiki system that can distinguish between a work in progress and an official release.

9.4.6.3   Weblogs

Weblogs ("blogs") are an interesting technology within the culture of Aerospace. Each expert currently has an established venue for publishing his or her thoughts and opinions (grounded in hard evidence). This established method of publishing includes several types of internal and externally directed report formats (including public release). Authoring data and publishing one's expertise in the form of formal corporate reports achieves the dual objectives of delivery and knowledge sharing. Aerospace publishes an "executive perspective" blog (from the office of the Chief Investment Officer) and a small collection of "expert perspective" blogs by noted organizational authorities.

Within a traditional office culture, blogs may be viewed with some skepticism. Although a major cultural shift must occur for readers to accept an author's direction to "read my blog" instead of "read my report," blogs are increasingly moving into the mainstream. Because blogs can provide an important reference point for personal opinion, they are gaining in value as a contributing component of the social network information within the workplace.

9.4.6.4   Podcasting

A podcast is a digital media file distributed over the Internet using syndication feeds for playback on PCs and portable media players. Through podcasts, online audio content is delivered "on demand" to the listener and automatically updated through a periodic interval.

Individuals have been drawn to podcasts as the means to distribute their own radio-style shows, but as the popularity of the media grew, podcast use has branched into other areas. Other uses of podcasts include the delivery of music, talk show content, news, stories, and training sessions. A popular example is *iTunes U*, which enables higher education institutions to provide audio and video content to their students. Presentations, performances, lectures, and tours are just a few examples of the type of content that can be provided through this digital format. Large corporations such as Microsoft and IBM have also utilized podcasts to support corporate training and the sharing of customer stories.

One initiative at Aerospace is to provide on-demand training through short video podcasts. In collaboration with The Aerospace Institute, which governs corporate training, the Knowledge Management Office will develop community-based training sessions, briefings, and similar content that will be broadcast to the company. Additionally, other presentations and video sessions created by other groups in the company can also be served through this media. Podcasting will serve as yet another platform to communicate to employees.

Will knowledge delivery via podcasting technology be effective at Aerospace? While Generation-Xers and Millennials do not comprise the majority of the company demographic, their experience and effective use of rich-media applications requires that consideration be given to podcasting as a knowledge delivery format. Both the advantages and disadvantages of using podcasting for knowledge sharing and communication must be examined. The portability of the content is a major plus. The ability to play audio and video podcasts in computers as well as through portable media players enables users to carry their knowledge assets with them at all times. This gives employees the ability to spontaneously share presentations stored in their iPod with coworkers in another building. Employees can also listen to the CEO's annual report while running on a treadmill, or watch training videos while standing in line at the airport. Corporate learning and communication are no longer restricted to attendance at a formal class or briefing. Podcasting expands the ability to provide employees with different styles of learning and presentations. On the downside, since podcasts are an audio digital feed, they are sequential and cannot be searched. A major challenge that faces distribution of knowledge via podcasting is the "new technology" factor. As with anything that is new, this is something that employees will have to be introduced to, trained to use, and convinced to integrate into their established work routine. While the members of the workforce that are culturally close to the social procedures of Generation Xers and Millennials may be able to accommodate podcasting without much disruption, broader application across the enterprise may be difficult.

Aerospace still has several issues to consider in order to advance the idea of podcasting for the enterprise. The company is experimenting locally in the knowledge management area within the various communities. Localized training snippets and community-building briefings are created as an initial deployment. If these efforts are successful, Aerospace will branch out in stages to capture meetings and briefings in podcasts. At a more mature stage of development podcasting can be integrated with the company's formal training institution.

9.4.7 Knowledge Retention via Storytelling

Storytelling is an important component of knowledge development, sharing, and retention at Aerospace. It allows for recent employees to learn from seasoned contributors. Since experience and "corporate memory" are so important to the company's mission, this is a key knowledge retention and transfer activity. Aerospace conducts storytelling in multiple venues:

■ *Our Place in Space (OPIS) Series*: This is a forum open to all Aerospace employees, in which key contributors to a specific mission area tell about their activities. Examples of topics discussed are: Global Positioning System (GPS), Launch, System Engineering, Developmental Planning, Satellite Communication, and other programs and activities. Some of the discussions focus on the current state of a program or technology. Others focus on specific contributions during a particular era of a program. It is fascinating to learn both the history and the subject matter from the individuals who made it happen. It is interesting to note that OPIS was originally intended for support staff, and over time developed a far broader audience that includes the technical staff and company executives.

▪ *Storytelling in the Library*: This series is dedicated exclusively to retired Aerospace leaders telling an audience during lunchtime about their career and Aerospace as it existed during their tenure. Guest speakers have included former CEOs and presidents, as well as executive staff (vice presidents) with a variety of responsibilities throughout the company. These well-attended storytelling sessions are very informal, and provide an opportunity to look at the history and evolution of Aerospace, as well as demonstrate impressive career paths to inspire the next generations.

▪ *Storytelling with our Publications—Crosslink*: Aerospace is committed to publishing *Crosslink* magazine [http://www.aero.org/publications/crosslink/index.html], which documents major areas of interest twice a year. This high-quality publication has covered topics such as Developing Our Technical Workforce, Mission Assurance, Navigation, Communication, Systems Engineering, Remote Sensing, Launch, Weather Satellites, Testing, Ground Systems, and Radiation and Space. The journal contains high-quality peer-reviewed articles that cover each area. Thus far, 17 issues of *Crosslink* have been published. Key contributors to the respective areas are highlighted, providing yet another reference point for others to identify subject matter experts and providing public recognition for the magazine's key contributors.

▪ *Contributing to Global Publications and Events*: All Aerospace staff are encouraged to publish within their professional communities in order to share accomplishments with the external world in the open domain. These publications include those sponsored by professional societies such as American Institute on Aeronautics and Aerospace (AIAA), Institute on Electrical Engineering and Electronics (IEEE), Association for Computing Machinery (ACM), American Physical Society (APS), and others. All of these publications become part of the public domain record and serve to educate Aerospace employees as well as facilitate dialogue with our global peers.

▪ *Hosting Professional Conferences*: In addition to Aerospace MTS attending multiple global conferences, Aerospace has taken the lead in hosting a number of conferences at or near Aerospace offices [http://www.aero.org/conferences/]. These conferences include the Ground Systems Architectures Workshop (GSAW), Spacecraft Thermal Control, Systems Engineering and Risk Management, Space Power, Space Testing, Space Parts, and many more. Currently approximately 15 conferences are organized and hosted by Aerospace.

9.5   Lessons Learned in Knowledge Retention

9.5.1   *A Company Library Is a Necessity for a Modern Knowledge Organization*

For almost 50 years, Aerospace has delivered knowledge as its sole product. When the company was formed in 1960, the knowledge stewardship topic was front and center. It was assumed that the knowledge delivered would be based on past experiences and current science; retaining past experiences was therefore a founding intention of the company. While document management has moved from paper to digital formats, the Aerospace library has always played a vital role in the retention of past knowledge. Although the library staff has "been there from the beginning" in relationship to processes and procedures, keeping records that can provide the basis for derivative works is a job function that spans the entire company. Subject area experts often are called upon to provide a discriminating view of material and to qualify the current context and conditions for which past written knowledge has merit.

9.5.2   *Knowledge Is Fragile and Needs Constant Tuning*

One thing that has become increasingly difficult to manage, as the breadth and depth of knowledge expands, is the stewardship of past knowledge. Those who claim participation within the knowledge management discipline are keenly aware that knowledge is fragile. As time advances, so do technology and the complexity of space-based systems. Knowledge stewardship is focused on moving the wisdom of the past into the context of the present (and future). The maintenance function around knowledge taxes the limited resources of the experts and precludes the broad-based proactive "update of old knowledge into new context" that would be the basis for a perfect solution to the knowledge management problem. Stated more simply, if there were a way of putting all of the lessons of the past into the context of current and future need in an automated way (with limited human thought required to update), the knowledge management problem would be solved for the most part. Since this is a world of finite human capital resources, those resources must be spent wisely, which requires making a top priority of maintenance around the most appropriate knowledge assets. Attending to "knowledge updates" (see Figure 9.10) has been driven by a need to put a specific element of historical knowledge into modern context. For example, the procedures for battery cycling and maintenance for space vehicles on orbit has followed a somewhat similar protocol over the years, but that protocol has required tuning and adjustment to extend the life cycle of space system batteries that are manufactured from different components than those used years earlier.

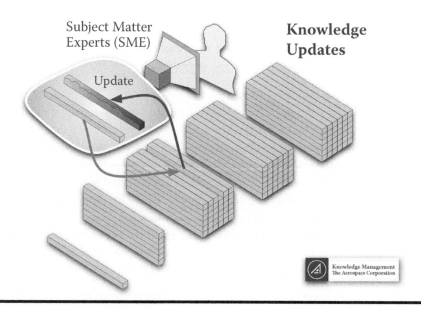

Figure 9.10 Knowledge Updates (From *Knowledge Management at The Aerospace Corporation—A 50 Year Journey*, p. 35. Copyright 2008 by The Aerospace Corporation. With permission.)

9.5.3 The Soft Stuff is the Hard Stuff

Knowledge management is not limited to information systems (IS) and technology. In fact, the most challenging aspects of successful knowledge management strategies deal with organizational behavior and the successful formation of teaming and business processes. It has been shown over the years that successful deployment of IS must always incorporate business processes and the IS tools in a seamless fashion. In fact, the deployment of IS in various organizations typically demonstrates a bimodal distribution, where deployment either wildly succeeds or fails miserably. The discriminator in many cases has been the degree to which the IS was integrated with the workflow, adopted by the workforce, and streamlined into the business process. For decades, experiences at Aerospace have reinforced these findings.

As discussed earlier, Aerospace has established CoPs and CoIs as part of its knowledge management strategy. While the CoIs are less formal, the CoPs pertain to the core mission of Aerospace and enjoy a formal governance structure, as discussed above. Some examples of CoPs that Aerospace supports are Knowledge Stewards, Laser Communication, Knowledge Management, Software Acquisition, Software Engineering/Architecture, Space Networks, Spectrum Management, Mission Assurance, Industrial Base, Space Policy, Complex Systems, and Operationally Responsive Space. CoPs members have regular meetings, organize their content within AeroLink, the company's knowledge depository, and enjoy high-level sponsorship by senior management.

Despite this, the major challenge that Aerospace has experienced within the initial period of deployment has to do with the adoption of the new organizational paradigm. The workforce is embracing the CoP paradigm with some trepidation. The CoPs are a new structure, spanning across traditional organizations. In addition, CoPs do not have their own source of funding; hence their operations and influence are working to gain traction. Company leadership provides some support from the corporate strategic initiatives, as well as from funding provided by the Knowledge Management Office. The ultimate goal at Aerospace is that customers would seek out the CoPs to perform various activities and deliver specific products. So far, these activities are performed mostly through the traditional organizational structure. This tension between the traditional organization and the new CoPs is likely to prevail for some time, as the company strives to achieve the right balance among CoPs, knowledge management operations, and the traditional organizational structure.

9.6 Summary

As system complexity increases, knowledge stewardship is becoming increasingly difficult. Keeping a complete record of the past encompasses more than just managing an ever-expanding digital history. Aerospace has been an effective steward of past experience, even when that experience was retained as a sort of corporate memorabilia.

References

1. APQC Knowledge Retention and Transfer Benchmarking Study 2007.
2. "Briefing: Using wikis at the National Research Council, Canada," *Knowledge Management Review*, 10(4), (Sept./Oct. 2007), 6–7.
3. Wikipedia (2007), "Arbitration," 8 Dec. 2007, http://en.wikipedia.org/wiki/Wikipedia:Arbitration_Committee.
4. Wikipedia (2007), "Wikipedia: Editorial oversight and control," 9 Dec. 2007, http://en.wikipedia.org/wiki/Wikipedia:Editorial_oversight_and_control.
5. Wikipedia (2007), "Wikipedia: Mediation Committee," 10 Dec. 2007 http://en.wikipedia.org/wiki/Mediation_Committee.

Chapter 10

Knowledge Retention: The Future

Today's Generation Yers are often quoted as saying that their success depends on their connections. Through the myriad of social networking sites, people are finding other individuals and new ways to "link in" with others. Additionally, through blogs and online communities, people are sharing knowledge in these different forums. And this will continue to expand. Look at Microsoft's relationship with Facebook, Google's acquisition of YouTube, and Rupert Murdoch's acquisition of MySpace; major companies are realizing the potential of social networking and targeted online advertising. A simple case in point is one undergraduate student advertising a college dinner event by putting a short video on YouTube and telling his Facebook contacts/addresses about it. Within 2 days of doing so, there were 230 attendees at the function. The point here is that connections with others and the sharing of knowledge between these individuals will continue to grow through social networking and collaborative digital mechanisms.

So, how does this relate to knowledge retention activities for the future? Through these informal networks, the knowledge sharing and transfer process is enhanced. The people-to-people cyber-connections allow for the possibility of more timely knowledge flows and at just-in-time situations.

Knowledge retention will continue to be a critical issue for many organizations in the years ahead. With the demographics showing approaching retirements of the baby boomer generation, a potential for a knowledge bleed effect could result. To ensure against this phenomenon happening, organizations need to have a knowledge retention and overarching human capital strategy in effect. This will contribute to proper workforce development and succession planning activities for the organization so that a knowledge drain will be minimized. Knowledge retention activities and policies need to be institutionalized throughout the organization so that proper transitioning can occur when people leave the organization. Perhaps having a policy whereby one cannot be promoted until he/she trains his/her successor should be used in an organization. Learning and knowledge sharing proficiencies should be part of the annual employee review process, and the recognition and reward structure should encourage people to share and transfer their knowledge.

"Age diversity" should be part of an organization's definition for diversity. Bringing back retirees for selected part-time positions or applying their knowledge as part of a knowledge preservation/oral history project could be important endeavors to bridge knowledge and skill gaps. Using retirees in mentoring roles could be extremely useful to the organization. Formal phased retirement programs in the organization would also allow the transitioning of positions and leveraging of knowledge as someone nears retirement age. The workforce of the future will continue to be a more "flexible workforce" than ever before. Through telecommuting, social networking, and Web-based technologies, tomorrow's employees will be more flexible in terms of working from home and in off-site locations. The mixture of employees, contractors, and consultants will continue to be diluted as more contractors and consultants will probably fill many positions in an as-needed basis. The full-time employees will serve as the primary managers and overseers of the projects. The contractors will carry out much of the work, and the consultants will be brought in for key pockets of expertise on a project-need basis.

Thus, when we think of "human capital" and the need for knowledge retention, it involves not only the full-time employees of the organization but also the "community" of people associated with the organization. This "community" could be international partners, universities, not-for-profits, contractors, consultants, third-party partners, customers, and other stakeholders. In developing a knowledge retention strategy, it will become ever more important to reach out to these various community members to help nurture, build, and preserve the human capital, structural capital, customer capital, and competitor capital comprising the intellectual capital of the organization. Hallmark, for example, reaches out to the general public through online communities to gather their ideas for new greeting cards. Through social networking and developing informal networks within the organization, knowledge flows will be created and new "knowledge networks" will be formed. Knowledge retention activities will also have to capture these knowledge networks in order to know who to go to for certain types of knowledge. Capturing an individual's knowledge base and social network should be part of a knowledge retention strategy.

10.1 Cross-Generational Knowledge Flows in Edge Organizations

Knowledge retention strategies should span across generational knowledge, particularly in edge organizations. An "edge organization" has the following properties: robustness, interoperability, competence, agility, shared awareness, decentralized knowledge and command, situational leadership, pull and smart, and a network-centric focus. In today's environment, edge organizations will become more commonplace. Part of the challenge in this area is examining how knowledge flows across generations in these edge organizations.

In examining the literature, cross-generational biases could relate to loyalty, making a contribution, work values, communications styles, gender, culture, ability to deal with ambiguity and change, autonomy/independence, and family values. Tacit knowledge transfer could relate to trust, organizational culture, societal cultural issues, early involvement, due diligence, reciprocity, values, motivation to share knowledge, and intrinsic worth of the knowledge to be conveyed.

Through 2007 research by Liebowitz et al. [1], funded by the Center for Edge Power at the Naval Postgraduate School and the DoD Command and Control Research Program, we start with the premise that, if knowledge enables action, then knowledge flows could be measured via the knowledge-based actions that they enable. We are thus interested in determining the goals and resulting actions that the edge-like teams hope to attain, and the knowledge that is sought to accomplish those goals. The research methodology used uni- and multigenerational edge-like teams with cross-generational knowledge flow and sharing questionnaires, observation/ethnographic analysis, interviews, and best practice research.

The following hypotheses were proven to be true:

- Cross-generational biases inhibit tacit knowledge transfer and decrease knowledge flows in edge organizations.
- Strong work and family values will facilitate tacit knowledge transfer and increase knowledge flows in edge organizations.
- Decreased communications will inhibit tacit knowledge transfer and decrease knowledge flows in edge organizations.
- Females act in a more collaborative manner than males, thereby increasing trust and tacit knowledge transfer, resulting in an increase of knowledge flows in edge organizations.
- A lack of interpersonal trust will result in reduced tacit knowledge transfer and decreased knowledge flows in edge organizations.
- Informal networks will result in an increase in tacit knowledge transfer and increased knowledge flows in edge organizations.

- Organizational and societal cultural barriers will decrease tacit knowledge transfer and decrease knowledge flows in edge organizations.
- Motivation to share knowledge through being recognized and rewarded will increase tacit knowledge transfer and increase knowledge flows in edge organizations.
- Reciprocity and the worthiness of the knowledge conveyed will stimulate tacit knowledge transfer and increase knowledge flows in edge organizations.

This research was novel in that the combination of intergenerational differences, tacit knowledge transfer, and edge organizations had never been studied. The study had some limitations relating to sample size and in-depth case studies. Follow-on funded research is being conducted on: (1) how the type of knowledge sought affects the influence of cross-generational biases in knowledge flows in edge-like teams, and (2) what critical success factors determine whether edge-like teams will be productive in terms of cross-generational knowledge flows.

10.2   Knowledge Retention: Future Challenges

Organizations must think proactively in order to anticipate and adjust to changing internal and external conditions. Becoming a "learning organization" is an essential tenet for this agility and flexibility. In order to strive toward this goal, organizations must develop knowledge retention strategies as part of their overall human capital strategy. Critical at-risk knowledge should be captured and shared, along with important process-oriented knowledge that underpins the organization. Capturing subject domain knowledge aligned with the strategic mission of the organization should also be conducted, as well as capturing the strategic and relationship knowledge embedded in the organization.

Part of the "knowledge retention challenge" will be that some leaders in the organization may have a short-term view in terms of making their mark on the organization. Knowledge retention and knowledge management initiatives often have a longer-term focus and transcend the organization. Investing in these longer-term initiatives will be crucial for the longevity of the organization. Measuring the intangible assets in the organization, as related to the organization's bottom line, is needed and will continue to be a challenge for some organizations.

Adjusting the recognition and reward system in the organization will also be important to encourage a knowledge sharing culture. In the spirit of sharing and transferring knowledge, employees will look toward the recognition and reward structure to encourage this behavior. Promoting a vision for change and collaboration as the de facto standard will be important elements for today's organizations to succeed in the future. Senior leadership's commitment and active involvement in human capital and knowledge retention endeavors are critical success factors for organizational longevity.

The naysayer of knowledge retention efforts may feel that "past consideration is no consideration." However, the institutional memory of the firm can help prevent going down the wrong paths and reinventing the wheel. Learning from others and from their best practices might result in increasing worker productivity and organizational effectiveness. Optimally, knowledge retention should not be conducted a few weeks before the individual leaves, but rather should be applied at least 2 to 3 years before the individual leaves (or even better, from day one of the individual's tenure in the organization, as no one really knows when they might leave an organization).

The future looks bright for those organizations that understand the changing work patterns of today's employees, the potential knowledge bleed effect based on societal demographics, and the importance of social networking and collaboration for knowledge creation. Developing and maintaining relationships and an appreciation for the "world being flat" are important tenets for today's organizations to be successful for tomorrow. As we close this chapter, knowledge retention strategies and solutions, as those proposed in this book, will become paramount toward achieving success in an increasingly competitive environment.

References

1. Liebowitz, J., N. Ayyavoo, H. Nguyen, D. Carran, and J. Simien (2007), "Cross-Generational Knowledge Flows in Edge Organizations," *Industrial Management & Data Systems Journal*, Vol. 107, No. 8, Emerald Publishing.

Index

A

After-action reviews (AARs), 12, 23–24, 42
  and continuous learning, 48
  at DTE energy, 24
  in military, 23, 48
Age diversity, 116
Attention Factor, 7–8
Attrition, 1, 2
  knowledge loss, 59–60
  lessons learned, 47
  lost business opportunities, 57, 58
  and organizational prestige, 57
  profiles, 3
  sources of, 74
Audits, 8, 30; *see also* Surveys

B

Best practices, 2, 28, 42; *see also* Lessons
      learned
  at DaimlerChrysler, 22
  of using retirees, 44–46
Biases, 5, 117
Blogs, 3, 24, 104, 108, 115
Brain drain, 57
Buddy system, 2, 44

C

Career transitions, 45
Change management, 2

Cheat sheets, 9, 21, 43
Codification, 3, 6, 12, 28
CoIs, *see* Communities of interest (CoIs)
Collaboration, 11, 90, 92, 117
Communications, 11, 109, 117
Communities of interest (CoIs), 102
Communities of practice (CoPs), 11, 75,
      76, 101
  metrics, 103
  peer review, 102
  setting positions, 102
  wisdom process, 101–102
Competency management, 2
Consultants, 4, 28, 45, 116
Content management systems, 4
Contextual knowledge, 78
Contingent workers, 45
Continuous learning, 27, 48, 53
Contractors, 28, 45, 116
CoPs, *see* Communities of practice (CoPs)
Core competencies, 8, 22, 51, 88
Corporate culture, 45, 46
  of continuous learning, 48
  of knowledge sharing, 2
Corporate memory, 6, 20, 109
Critical "at-risk" knowledge, 13, 42, 59,
      72, 118
  calculation, 7
  people who possess, 42

D

Decision-making, 13, 15
  in groups, 17

rationale template, 16
Declarative knowledge, 78
Digital library, 92
Document management, 104

E

Edge organizations, 117–118
Emeriti programs, 4
Employees, *see* Workforce
Exit interviews, 2, 5, 21–22
Expertise, 6; *see also* Subject matter experts
 (SMEs)
 capturing, 10, 72
 locating, 28, 43, 98–99
 nature of, 76, 77
Explicit knowledge, 28, 59, 77

F

Focus groups, 17

G

Golden Gem, 28–29
Graybeards, 6, 12, 20
Grayout factor, 55–58

H

Human capital management, 5, 115, 116
 and demographics, 1, 73, 74, 115
 key principles, 45
 pillars of, 2
Human resources, 5; *see also* Human capital
 management

I

Information technology (IT); *see also* Intranets
 infrastructure, 9
 integration with workflow, 112

new technology factor, 109
 software, 43, 48
Innovation, 25, 47, 49, 51, 59
Institutional memory, *see* Corporate memory
Internet, *see* Weblogs; Wikis
Interviews, 8, 15–17; *see also* Exit interviews
 observation, 17
 oral histories, 19–21
 organizational narratives, 15, 42
 protocol, 17
 questions, 27–28
 scenario building, 15
 structure, 17
 templates, 16
 videotaping, 42–43
Intranets, 9
 memory aids, 21
 video repository, 43
IT, *see* Information technology (IT)

J

Job rotation, 28
Job sharing, 28

K

Knowledge; *see also* Critical "at-risk"
  knowledge; Knowledge flows;
  Knowledge loss;
  Knowledge sharing
 accuracy, 24
 analysis, 31–32
 base, 4, 56
 delivery, 49, 108, 109
 dissemination, 12, 49, 50, 89, 93
 gain, 59
 gaps in, 2, 5
 needs, 39
 resources, 34–36
 search, 98
 stewardship, 87, 88, 91
 technical, 22
 transfer, 117–118
 types of, 7, 78
 updates, 111
 use, 36–37

worth, 56, 101, 117
Knowledge Availability (KA), 7
Knowledge capture, *see* Codification;
    Personalization
Knowledge creation, 2, 6, 12, 101, 119
Knowledge flows, 2, 5, 40
    bidirectional, 27–28
    cross-generational, 117–118
    in edge organizations, 117
    timeliness, 115
Knowledge harvesting, 57, 76–78
    elicit stage, 81–82
    evaluation, 83–84
    find stage, 80
    focus stage, 79–80
    lessons learned about, 85
    organize, package stage, 82
    stages, 78
Knowledge loss, 3
    calculating, 55–58
    cost of turnover, 57
    due to downsizing, 59
    "grayout" factor, 55–58
    intangibles, 58
    positive gain from, 58–59
    risk assessment, 59–60
Knowledge management
    attrition profiles, 3
    goals, 9
    infrastructure, 9
    initiatives, 9, 76, 93–94, 118
    and lessons learned, 51
    performance measures, 11–12
    strategy alignment, 5
Knowledge retention programs, 41, 43
    capture process, 42–43
    getting started, 29
    management support for, 113
    measuring effectiveness, 25
    obstacles to, 4–6
    participation in, 46, 47, 105
    people, 41–42
    pillars of, 26
    technology, 43
    toolset, 75–76
Knowledge Severity (KS), 7
Knowledge sharing, 37–38; *see also* Surveys
    culture of, 2, 51
    and motivation, 117, 118
    as part of employee reviews, 116
    proficiencies, 12

reciprocity, 118
    and reciprocity, 5, 117, 118
    safeguarding, 93
    tenets for success, 51

L

Learning, 6, 14, 109; *see also* Lessons learned;
        Training
    continuous, 48, 53
    life cycle, 75
    styles, 13
Learning organization, 11, 118
Lessons learned, 2, 4, 11, 23, 42; *see also*
        After-action reviews (AARs)
    on attrition, 47
    effectiveness, 49
    interview template, 16
    and knowledge management, 51
    and knowledge sharing, 51
    metrics, 52–53
    from private sector, 46–48
    processes, 48–52
    proof of concept, 52–53
    push vs. pull systems, 10, 49–50
    recognitions, 50
    search and retrieval, 52, 53
    software, 48
    system user responses, 48–49
    through project life cycle, 49
    validating, 50
    value-added, 12
Libraries, 89–90, 111

M

Meetings
    open, 11
Mentoring, 2, 4, 26, 44
    at John Hopkins University, 19
    as metric, 11
    NASA program, 17, 18
Mentoring program, 17, 18
Metrics
    for knowledge management strategy,
        11–12
    lessons learned, 52–53

for mentoring, 11
Motivation, *see* Recognitions; Rewards
Multimedia assets, 43

O

Online communities, 4, 10, 11, 24, 44; *see also*
    Intranets; Weblogs; Wikis
Oral histories, 19–21, 116
Organizational network analysis (ONA)
  brokering roles, 63–64
  case example, 64–67
  and knowledge retention, 72
  survey, 67–71
Organizations
  and community, 116
  competitive edge, 4, 5, 25, 58
  downsizing, 59, 74
  efficiency, 25, 119
  goals, 1, 9, 45, 76, 80
  growth, 25
  informal, 26
  longevity, 118
  strategic mission, 118
Outsourcing, 59

P

Performance management, 2, 45
Personal contact files, 43
Personalization, 3, 6, 10, 12, 28
Phased retirement, 26, 28, 44, 116
Podcasting, 108–109
Procedural knowledge, 78
Process knowledge, 7, 118
  protocol "bibles," 22
Process management, 22
Program management, 22

R

Recognitions, 5, 26–27, 118
Relationship knowledge, 2, 7
Retirees
  associations, 45
  bringing back, 4, 28, 29, 45

executives, 45
part-time, 44
as temporary workers, 44
from universities, 46
Retirement programs, 26, 28, 44, 116
Rewards, 5, 26–27, 118; *see also* Recognitions

S

Social knowledge, 78
Social networks, 2, 13, 22, 115, 116; *see also*
    Online communities;
    Organizational network analysis
    (ONA)
  analysis, 42
  online, 24
  software, 48
Statement of work, 29–30
Storytelling, 19–21, 28, 42, 109–110
Strategic knowledge, 7, 41, 65
Subject matter domain, 7, 41, 65, 118
Subject matter experts (SMEs), 10, 14, 31, 75,
  78
Succession planning, 9, 25, 43, 55, 115
Surveys, 8, 33–34
  knowledge flow, 40
  knowledge needs, 39
  knowledge resources, 34–36
  knowledge use, 36–37
  sharing, 37–38
  tools used, 38
  training, 38

T

Tacit knowledge, 15, 28, 77
  codification, 46
  transfer, 60, 117–118
Technology, *see* Information technology (IT)
Telecommuting, 116
Temporary workers, 44
Training, 60, 75
  for managers, 44
  for mentors/mentees, 18, 19
  on-demand, 108
  podcasting, 108, 109
  successor before promotion, 116

survey on, 38
tutorials, 19
Trust
    benevolence-based, 4
    competence-based, 4
    and knowledge transfer, 117
Turnover, 38, 57, 82

U

Unretirement, 45

V

Value creation, 25, 47, 49, 51, 59
Value network analysis, 57

W

Weblogs, 3, 24, 104, 108, 115
Wikis, 3, 24, 93
    benefits of, 104–105
    bulletin board type, 105
    governance, 106, 107
    peer review, 107
    quality of content, 106
    for team projects, 105–106
Workforce
    competency, 76
    contingent workers, 45
    development, 9, 25, 43, 75, 115
    flexible, 44, 116
    junior employees, 27
    misclassification, 45
    new hires, 74, 75, 76
    older employees, 27, 44
    recruitment, 44
    training, 38, 44

For Product Safety Concerns and Information please contact our EU representative GPSR@taylorandfrancis.com Taylor & Francis Verlag GmbH, Kaufingerstraße 24, 80331 München, Germany

T - #0017 - 230425 - C0 - 234/156/8 [10] - CB - 9781420064650 - Gloss Lamination